EXPONENTIAL
series

AND

The Gathered and Scattered Church

Hugh Halter and Matt Smay

ZONDERVAN®

ZONDERVAN.com/
AUTHORTRACKER
follow your favorite authors

LEADERSHIP NETWORK®

ZONDERVAN

AND: The Gathered and Scattered Church
Copyright © 2010 by Hugh Halter and Matt Smay

This title is also available as a Zondervan ebook.
Visit www.zondervan.com/ebooks.

This title is also available in a Zondervan audio edition.
Visit www.zondervan.fm.

Requests for information should be addressed to:

Zondervan, *Grand Rapids, Michigan* 49530

Library of Congress Cataloging-in-Publication Data

Halter, Hugh, 1966 –.
    AND: the gathered and scattered church / Hugh Halter and Matt Smay.
        p. cm. – (Exponential series)
      ISBN 978-0-310-32585-7 (softcover)
      1. Church. 2. Church growth. I. Smay, Matt, 1972 – II. Title. III. Title: Gathered and
scattered church.
    BV600.3.H355 2010
    254'.5 – dc22   2009053278

Published in association with the literary agency of WordServe Literary Group, Ltd., 10152 S. Knoll Circle, Highlands Ranch, CO 80130.

Cover design: Rob Monacelli
Interior design: Matthew Van Zomeren

Printed in the United States of America

10 11 12 13 14 15 16 17 18 19 /DCI/ 18 17 16 15 14 13 12 11 10 9 8 7 6 5 4 3 2 1

Again, to our wives, Cheryl and Maren, and our kids, Ryan, Alli, Mckenna, Maegan, and Madison, who have given up a lot of precious family time to allow this story to be told. We are grateful for your sacrifice with us. Hopefully, normal life may resume soon.

To the Church, and the Head of the Church, Christ our Lord.

Contents

Thanks

WHEREAS *The Tangible Kingdom* and the *TK Primer* was our story to share, *AND* happened because of many others who inspired us through their stories. To the people listed below, we are deeply thankful for your friendship, encouragement, and collaboration on *AND*.

To our Missio Team Leaders throughout North America who model the AND and who give their time apprenticing missional leaders, we thank Gary Swabey, Ron Schlitt, Tim Colemen, Brandon Hatmaker, Tyler Johnson, Phil Grizzle, Lance Ford, Daniel Allen, and Lou Braun. In close alliance with Missio, we also want to acknowledge Cam Roxburgh and Alan Hirsch, and those who serve with FORGE/Canada.

We thank our agent and friend Greg Johnson, and Kevin Tracy, Caleb Seeling, Allie Harding, and Andrew Taylor for hours of effort on the manuscript. We also thank Church Resource Ministries for generously stewarding Missio's development and calling, and for "sending" us well.

To Todd Wilson, Exponential, and our new friends at Zonder-van and Leadership Network, we thank you for your desire to see the church come together around God's great mission.

To Adullam, our community of faith, thanks for your flexibil-ity, your challenge, and your unrelenting unwillingness to simply "go to church."

Foreword

ONE OF GOD'S MOST AWESOME DISPLAYS of creativity happens during the autumn season. God brings out a variety of brilliant colors — oranges, reds, and yellows — as the leaves change and transition from the shades of summer green. After the brilliance of these autumn colors, the leaves die and float to the ground.

Most people collect them in piles and dispose of them. However, there are occasions when the carefully gathered leaves get scattered back to the wind. And kids are usually the culprits. Children just love to gather hundreds of leaves in piles, rolling in them, jumping in them, throwing them around ... then scattering them back into the yard again.

Of course, parents who have worked hard at gathering piles don't always appreciate seeing them scattered, but occasionally, they too will join in the fun. Yet joining in the game requires a shift in their thinking, recognizing that leaves can be more than something we gather to throw away — they can also be a source of joy as they are scattered back to the wind by playful children.

God's brilliant creativity can also be seen in the beautifully diverse body of his Son, Jesus Christ. The church is beautiful when God's people are gathered together in worship. But in addition to the beauty of the gathered body, there is another side to the beauty of the church. There is a profound beauty we can see and experience when God's Spirit stirs the gathered body of Christ, scattering them outward to the ends of the earth.

God has always shown a desire to be in fellowship with human beings and to provide for their needs. Sadly, that desire was spoiled through our disobedience in the garden. After God scattered Adam and Eve by casting them out of the garden, we see a recurring pattern that unfolds in the Scriptures: a cycle of scattering and gathering. The human race gathers together in pride at the Tower of Babel, and God scatters them. People from every nation under heaven gather on the day of Pentecost to hear about God's mighty deeds, and they are scattered back to their peoples to bring the message of the gospel. The early church gathered to celebrate God's redemptive work through Jesus, yet they were soon scattered by persecution and the move of God's Spirit.

Just as love and marriage go together (you really can't have a good one without the other), gathering and scattering go together. That's just the way God set things up! He chose to gather a people to himself from among the scattered peoples of the world.

And he is still at work today, scattering his gathered church to the ends of the earth. He scatters us to proclaim his glory and his goodness among those that haven't yet been gathered. If we want to honor God's intentions, we must recognize that it's not really about gathering *or* scattering. It's about *both*. For the most part, the church in North America has the gathering part down pretty good. It's the scattering that we need to work on.

Over the last several years, I have written about putting the revitalization of the church **AND** being missional together. I've sought to champion the idea that the mission of the church is really about making more **AND** better followers. Whether your church is a mega, multi, or a mini, the reality is that God is using each of these models — and the people in these churches — to advance his kingdom. God is the one who calls us, gathers us, shapes us, and sends us out again — regardless of the size or structure of our church.

In addition, he is the one who owns the church. The church, in all of her shapes, sizes, and models and with all of her flaws and unusual fragrances, belongs to him. Jesus paid the redemptive price for a people who would reflect the radiance of his glory and the reality of his presence to every tongue, tribe, and nation.

Matt, Hugh, and I agree that the church needs to become more missional, that we need to learn how to make more *and* better disciples, and that we need to do a better job of scattering our gathered bodies back into the world, a world that desperately needs to know the truth about God. We do all of this to reach the nations and bring glory to our redeeming God. That's the message of this book.

These two missional leaders have provided a resource that will help followers of Jesus, church leaders, and local churches learn how to better express the missional movements of gathering AND scattering in the body of Jesus Christ. Consider the biblical principles and practices they describe as they flesh out what God has been doing in their lives and the communities of Adullam. Then, decide what thoughts, ideas, and strategies God might want you to use in your life as a follower of Jesus and in your local church context.

My hope is that God will help all of us learn and grow in our understanding of the redemptive movement of God as he gathers and scatters the body of Christ in the days ahead. I hope too that his name and fame might be exalted among the nations.

— Ed Stetzer
President, LifeWay Research
www.edstetzer.com

Introduction

A Church the World Is Asking For

"WHAT IS WITH THE CHURCH?"

How many times has your heart asked your head this question? As I write this, I'm flying home from a week's journey in Scotland and Ireland. Matt and I spoke to collegiate groups, missionaries, new church leaders, and students at a number of Bible institutes. About half the leaders we spoke to work in more formal ministry settings, while the other half were just simple blokes, peasants, business leaders, and pub-dwellers. We traveled there to talk about the church. As we cautiously tiptoed into their context to offer a bit of our wisdom, I found myself struck by the irony of two greenhorns from the States trying to explain church to people who have been recovering from ecclesial traditions for ten times as long as my country has been in existence. Edifices and symbols of Christendom tap you on the shoulder at every turn and whisper words of warning.

Like many Americans, I can quickly dismiss it as a different culture and think, "No, that can't happen to us." But this time it was different. I've been increasingly disturbed by the reality that the American church has its coordinates locked in on being culturally negligent and irrelevant. I envision a future where the spiritually hungry look everywhere *but* the church for help — where the church becomes like the Salvation Army, and the culture tolerates our presence as long as we are content to collect a little spare change and help a few homeless; where we become a defensive, minority political force instead of a blessed army of soul-changers; where we continue to be known for what we *don't do* instead of what we *are doing* for the greater good of humanity.

Taking my church consultant hat off for minute, I will also acknowledge that one of my main concerns is for my own children. I wonder if my daughters (who are now fourteen and fifteen years old) will be able to find even a glimmer of hope in the idea of church. Or will they be in the same situation as the students in Glasgow, Scotland? In a city of almost a million people, the local leaders in Glasgow can only think of a handful of churches that have any reasonable witness — and the largest church is around a hundred people.

In the once spiritually vibrant Scotland, as we worked with local leaders, we often spent our down time relaxing in two churches. But these weren't places of worship. Both buildings were built as Reformed enclaves in the fifteenth century, and they now serve as pubs. Really nice pubs, to be sure! I know it's fashionable to make jokes about past churches being the center of drinking activity in the town, but I really do think it's pretty impressive that these church buildings have lasted hundreds of years. I doubt any of us think we could really keep the ole' First Baptist alive that long. Few churches in America last past their second birthday.

During our time in Ireland, the scene was even more colorful. Missionaries who had been in Dublin for twenty-five years expressed that they had tried and participated in every possible angle, alignment, or action plan they could find, but were still seeing little fruit. Ireland now has an evangelical presence of little more than 1 percent. We visited ancient monastic sites that had once been relevant and active faith communities and castles where men and women had once died for their Christocentric beliefs; and we even visited the Guinness Brewery—where we learned that Guinness, a benevolent Christian businessman, had created beer so that the townspeople would stop drinking whiskey. Now there's a creative outreach program!

Signs of past spiritual fervor were visible everywhere, but the stench of spiritual confusion, abuse, anger, and hopelessness was now wafting through every street corner, neighborhood, and public house. We did meet with a remnant of Christ followers, but none of them really had much hope in the church. Most of them were trying to avoid the present paradigms of church ministry in a desperate effort to put distance between the widespread perception of organized religion and their genuine faith in Jesus.

Sitting in the airplane at 30,000 feet, processing all that I had experienced on this trip, I began to ponder my calling and those questions we don't think often about. I wondered if my life would actually make any difference. I wondered if my leadership in our church in Denver would contribute to the continued decline of Christianity. Or would the tension of doing things differently help to start a new possibility for people?

I began to ask God fresh questions about what it meant for me to be faithful to him, about the nature of God's reign on the earth, about the extent of evil and its power to fight against God's ways, and about what life might feel like if the church were to continue on the current path. How much would it cost me if I chose to fight against the natural gravity and pressure of life and gave my all to him? Would the fruit be worth the pain? I began to think about the host of young leaders whom we've nurtured and have grown to love as much as our own kids. I wondered about their calling and the calling of tens of thousands of other young, altruistic passionaries who would love to change the world in the name of Christ, but who feel they have to go it alone and without a viable faith collective.

Normally, thinking about these things gets me a bit depressed, but as I stared into the blank four-inch TV screen in front of me, I was reminded of the creativity and power of God. I wondered what God could do with an entire generation who loves him but won't settle for stale church anymore. What could God do with an army of kingdom peasants who have no interest in safety, religion, or money, but who want to help people experience the presence of his kingdom in the here and now? While denominations struggle to survive, what might God do with relational networks of kingdom leaders who long to see something new happen in this generation?

I was immediately reminded of a meeting we had recently hosted in Denver, the day before we had left on the trip. We had called together a gathering of some of America's most intuitive incarnational church leaders. Some of these leaders were micro-practitioners who had found fruit serving God in the house church movement. Others were mega-church and multisite leaders. Just one table of leaders at this gathering represented pastoral influence over more than 40,000 people. Others who gathered with us were network leaders, denominational heavies, and mission agency reps. We met because we had become friends, and through strange, other-worldly connections, we were blessed to find people who were sniffing the same flower.

We were all attracted to the fragrance of collaboration — collaboration of kingdom, mission, incarnation, and movement. These were all successful, well-respected men and women representing a variety of ecclesial forms. All of them knew that they could easily rest on their laurels, coast along with business as usual, and neglect the bigger vision of the kingdom. But we were gathered together because we knew that the time had come for us to set aside the arguments over church forms and begin a new discussion about the more fundamental purpose of God's church.

These were leaders who were hungry for the *AND*.

A few months earlier we had attended a large pastors' conference in Dallas and had found ourselves stuck in the same old conversations about how to do church and which type of church is better. Everything was focused on the question of "how to do church." Since this was a large gathering, it was held at one of the larger suburban mega-churches in the area.

As Matt and I walked into the building, we were immediately taken aback by the size of the foyer. It was larger than the convention center in Portland, Oregon, where I had planted my first church! There was a three-tiered water fountain and a huge coffee and refreshment area that rivaled any Starbucks. The hallways were wide enough to drive a monster truck through, and they had a cool Swiss Family Robinson tree in the children's wing. Matt and I always enjoy seeing new venues; but as we looked at the building around us, I found myself wanting to critique, make jokes, deconstruct, do the math on how much I could accomplish by using this amount of money in different ways, and question whether disciples were really being made in this environment. Just for laughs I asked one of registration ladies when the next shuttle was available to take me to the restroom and if they rented Segways to help people get to the sessions on time. She didn't think it was funny.

During one of the breaks in the conference, I found myself "rest-rooming" next to the senior pastor, whom I had just seen on the jumbotron hosting the event. It is always awkward to stir up a kingdom conversation during the call of nature, but not wanting to miss an opportunity to schmooze, I made an attempt at conversation. Sensitively looking straight ahead, I said, "So ... nice restroom."

"Thanks," said the well-known pastor, also looking straight ahead.

Hmm, I thought to myself, *you gotta do better than that, Halter.*

As we moved from the porcelain relief area to the washbasins, I dove deeper. "Actually, this is a pretty nice building all around. Where did you get the idea for the cool fountain in the foyer? Do people ever raft down that thing?" I joked.

"I thought of it while taking a shower at home," he replied. "I just wanted to have a beautiful place for people to enjoy each other."

After a little more man-chat, I asked him if he had caught much flack from his congregation or from outsiders for spending so much money on the facility. "Nope, not really. This is Texas! We're not even the biggest church in the neighborhood." He then shared how the church had decided to give one dollar to overseas church planting for every dollar they spent on the church. The vision for supporting the work of missions so captured the hearts of church members that resources were easily raised and joyfully shared around the world.

As we continued talking, I noticed another voice inside my heart speaking up and arguing with the judgmental voice. The voice seemed to be acknowledging the goodness, maybe even the greatness of this leader and the viable ministry of this church. He was a humble, unassuming man, not apologetic or insecure about his church structure (even though it could easily double as a maintenance hangar for ten Boeing 767s). But he was also not boastful or proud or deluded into thinking his building was anything special. He was simply a godly servant and a faithful leader; it just so happened that God had called him to pastor a small suburb.

This story not only illustrates how quickly men can become friends in a restroom, but that there's more to the story of every church than you might think. At this event, I surmised that about half of the leaders were quite at home in the mega-world. They not only believe that mega-churches do good ministry, they authentically seem to enjoy working hard to provide excellent presentations, messages, and programs that fit any possible need or want. In a recent book on mega-churches, I read that though they were once thought to be in decline, these large ministries are continuing to grow in size, style, and success.

The newest evolution of the mega-movement is called "multisite." Classic mega-churches have grown into large centralized *structures*; multisite churches are able to grow even larger with a centralized *leadership team*. Instead of trying to get everyone under the same roof, church leaders sanction alternative gathering sites while maintaining cohesive vision and teaching through video-venue methods. There are many unique expressions within this model, but most multisite churches develop functional onsite pastoral teams or "campus pastors" that care for, assimilate, disciple, and organize people into small groups, while keeping the training, leadership development, administration, and teaching more centralized. There are multisite venues that cross state and international lines, and it seems only a matter of time before one pastoral team will franchise campuses that cross the blue seas and link 100,000 people under the teaching of a single person.

Like my knee-jerk judgment when entering the mega-zone, both of these expressions of "Big Church" have taken some pretty major heat over the last ten years. I liken the critique of the mega- and multisite movements to a big elephant that gets pecked to death by a dive-bombing flock of crows. The primary reason these ministries are disliked and critiqued is simply because they consume so many resources and seem to endorse uncritically a lifestyle of consumption. This type of church typically takes in a lot of money, uses up a lot of space, requires a lot of staff, seems to be based on the skills or charisma of a few leaders, fails to truly mobilize the ranks, and seems doomed to failure as generations change, values shift, and the economy weakens.

While talking to a Christian futurist during this mega-church conference, I learned that the majority of funding for most megachurches comes from the Boomer generation. These folks grew up with a high value for stability, and they generally equate a large building with sustainability. The bad news for these churches is that later generations don't necessarily share these values. We may have only another ten years at this level of financial commitment and available resources.

Another level of critique centers on health issues in the megachurch movement. Like a person who is overweight, could the size of the church eventually lead to health problems? Does this type of church actually make disciples? Is the ministry healthy, leading to kingdom fruit? The Willow Creek *Reveal* report that came out in 2008 only intensified the debate, as the country's most respected mega-pioneer, Bill Hybels, admitted that growing disciples weren't always the end result of all their attraction-based programs.

After my restroom dialogue with the mega-man, I sauntered my way down to the barista bar for some java and began a dialogue with the most prolific micro-dude of our time. This man has written extensively on the organic movement, whether it's a house church, a simple church, or a saturation church. He has studied the apostolic movement of these churches throughout the world, and he graciously gave me fifteen minutes of brilliant wisdom and passion for the decentralized, noninstitutional church. I learned that even though the mega-movement is on the rise, it's equaled in curiosity, dialogue, experimentation, and forms by people in the micro-camp.

These Lilliputian expressions of church tend to break away from centralized, facility-centered, program- and presentation-focused, attractional approaches. They focus instead on decentralized, relationally centered, incarnationally focused, missional approaches. Such churches choose not to base their methodology on money, buildings, leadership structures, traditional training models, or typical resourcing methods. In fact, they often feel that these issues are what hinder the *missio dei* ("mission of God"). They challenge contemporary understandings of what a disciple is and how one is made, and they often feel that traditional, attractional, consumer-oriented ways of church are actually hindering the process of making disciples. They believe that to make a disciple one must first remove the things that a consumer Christian or consumer seeker is consuming.

When they first hear the micro-lingo, many people intuitively think it sounds better. These are the people who tend to prefer an indigenous coffee house to a Starbucks, or a local hardware store over a Wal-Mart. For them, it just seems to be a more "moral" way of living. Just as Obama-mania made its living on the nebulous idea of change, this church deconstruction movement has been winning over the hearts of the masses.

Yet, the micro-church movement is not without its perils and remains vulnerable to some legitimate critiques. Micro-challengers often push back and encourage the critics of the mega-movement to quit talking a big game until they have proven their worth: "If you can't get more than eight people in your living room, and your evangelistic stats don't show any greater prowess, please don't get cranky with those of us who are trying to make disciples out of hundreds and thousands."

At a national organic church gathering, I led a breakout session called "Organic Church ... What If It Works?" I chose my title primarily because I was curious. I wanted to hear from some organic church leaders and see some pictures of success. How were these leaders navigating the opportunities that freedom outside the box afforded them? What were their struggles? I started out the session by asking them why they had come to the breakout. Why this particular session? As they went around the room, one by one, they started to share their own struggles and why they had left the "big church" in exchange for a chance to try "small church" ministry. Some spoke of the financial struggle of working a normal job and still having the energy left for ministry. Some shared that their spouses really missed corporate worship and the great programs once afforded them. Others lamented that although the ideas make sense on paper, maybe the organic church movement wasn't quite contextual for most of the people in their suburbs and cities. One leader likened the process of calling evangelicals to organic mission to trying to "sell rocks."

Although many leaders are intrigued by a decentralized, non-programmatic approach, they struggle to picture their life and ministry in this model. They question if the lack of structure is simply a front for laziness. The idea of a flattened, "non-leadership" leadership ethic sounds great — until you try to actually lead people somewhere. Many others were just honest about their disappointment: "Meeting in my living room with nine people for the next sixteen months isn't that inspiring." Others invariably ask, "What in the heck are we supposed to do with the kids?" while failing to see the good news in sending them downstairs to watch Veggie Tales.

Add to these ministry dilemmas the harsh reality that thousands of leaders have spent their entire lives training in attractional forms of church, and they now find it difficult at the age of forty to get a job working as a barista at Starbucks! Outside of knowing how to prepare a sermon, run a staff meeting, and meet with people for coffee, many vocational ministers struggle to enter the workforce with no marketable skills. Even those who secure employment quickly learn that work makes you tired, and the last thing you want to do after a day of work is be "incarnational." Heck, most leaders just want a bag of chips, a six-pack of something, and an hour of quiet to watch reruns of Seinfeld! Small definitely has its intrigue—the mobility, leanness, and lack of presentational pressure—but let's face it, it's hard to figure out how to live this way!

Of course, it's much easier to start a micro-church, but interestingly, we find that many gifted leaders struggle to keep it that way. When we coach house church leaders, we often ask them a simple question: "So what are you going to do if this thing works?"

What usually follows is a blank stare and a few cave man grunts. "Uh?"

"You know, what happens when your house fills up, and then another house, and then another? And what happens if the people want to all get together to actually see each other?"

"Well, uh ... I guess we'll figure out some way to get people together."

Often, micro-leaders begin to feel some responsibility to link smaller communities together and find ways to allow for meaningful corporate gatherings. Eventually, they find themselves staring at the ceiling at night wondering, "Have I just become another church?"

So what's the point of my lengthy diatribe on competing church forms? Well, to put it simply: maybe we shouldn't be competing with each other. Quite possibly, God may be growing weary of our deconstructive critiques guised in the covering of "strategy." Maybe our personal frustrations with our roles and our bad experiences with the church are due, to some extent, to our incessant search for the perfect church instead of honing in on what God cares about most. If you're wondering whom I sided with after meeting mega-man and micro-man—"Which church would you want to do, Halter?"—well, to be honest, I don't think it matters. In fact, I think it's the wrong question to ask. That's why we've written this book.

Matt and I pastor a church called "Adullam." Yes, it's an odd name, but it's biblical ... it means *refuge*. And after five years, I'm still not sure what type of church we are. If you've read the story of our Denver church in our book *The Tangible Kingdom* (Hoboken, NJ: Jossey-Bass, 2008), you may have initially thought we were another missional movement critiquing the *Mega-Church*. In our book, we share many incarnational stories of ministry happening in homes, pubs, and coffee shops, and because of that, some folk view us as *House Church* advocates. Because we share a story of a church happening naturally without any programs, others label us as a *Simple Church*. Still others, who know that we have larger gatherings, call us *Traditional Church*, while some tag us with the label *Contemporary Church/Post-Modern* because of our casual ways and because we occasionally light a candle. And on occasion, we read a blog or receive an email, suggesting we're a *cult*. If you ask people in Adullam what we are, my guess is that they would shrug their shoulders and call us *normal*.

When people push us for our "model," I generally say, "We're sort of a hybrid. We have a missionary thrust that forces us out of the church walls into a network of incarnational communities, but we also deeply value our collective calling, our corporate essence, and our consistent larger gatherings." Our website now articulates that Adullam is a "congregational network of incarnational communities." In other words, we are holding together two aspects of church that people seem to think can't go together.

The church is a beautiful mystery. Both mega- and micro-expressions have some perks and some pitfalls, strengths and weaknesses, as well as enemies and allies. Each side of the spectrum has a few examples of wild success as well as a much longer line of failed attempts and frustrated leaders. Picking one side or the other is *not* the right place to start. We need to move beyond the divide.

At some point, every leader questions their methods, laments how slow it is to produce a disciple, and wrings their hands over indifference and lethargy. Whether you are a mega-church pastor or a bivocational leader (or an unpaid saint), we all worry about resources. We get depressed that so much is spent on buildings and salaries (even if it's our own). We struggle to see how our biblical teaching makes any sense to a world that isn't really looking to come to church. We silently question our own calling, and although we can sound confident about our vision for church, we still wonder from time to time if what we're doing is really what Jesus would do.

The Scriptures are clear. God is the one who builds the church. In Acts 2, he turned a network of house churches into a mega-church, and in Acts 8 he allowed a centralized Hebrew church to be scattered all over the new world. On the one occasion he centralized a decentralized movement, and then later he decentralized a centralized movement.

It's time for us to stop asking the same old questions about *how* to do church, and instead ask *what* every church must be doing to honor God's biblical mandates. We'd like to introduce you to the subtle power of the **AND**.

The power of the AND is seen in churches of *all* sizes where:

⇨ there is a balance between gathering a community together AND scattering them into the world.

⇨ the right things are centralized AND the right things can be decentralized.

⇨ resources of people and money find a blessed balance between maintenance AND mission, survival AND sending, tradition AND innovation.

⇨ fans are turned into followers, disciples are made into apprentices, AND consumers become missionaries.

⇨ leaders influence according to the design of God instead of the whims of people or the pride associated with production.

⇨ old skills still matter AND new habits of mission take center stage.

⇨ you can have huge vision for thousands of people AND live life in deep community and communal witness.

⇨ your church learns to live a fluid organic Christianity AND has enough structure to provide for any level of growth God wants. (Remember, it's God who builds a church.)

⇨ you'll have to work hard, give up your life, AND have a blast!

As any church develops these ANDs, you'll be better positioned to influence those inside ranks AND those outside; your church will make sense in the burbs AND in the city, during financial recession AND in bull markets. You'll be able to start and steward a church if well resourced AND you'll be able to lead and live well without much help.

Most importantly, you'll be able to sleep at night, knowing that you are participating in God's church, which aligns with the greater call to make real disciples.

So if you are tired of judging, justifying, critiquing, and deconstructing; if you are unwilling to live with the stench of isolation, fear, and myopic vision; if you are ready to join the growing band of servants who love the church and who are working together to create a new waft of kingdom collaboration, then we invite you to come with us. Welcome to the opportunities of the AND.

CHAPTER 1

The Beautifully Sent Church

BEFORE I SHARE THIS NEXT THOUGHT, I feel compelled, out of my personal insecurity, to tell you that I'm a man ... a *real* man, a man's man. I like mixed martial arts. I often eat an entire Chipotle burrito with extra meat. I enjoy fishing, hunting, and taking the top off my Jeep Wrangler during 2:00 p.m. lightning storms in Denver. I don't eat glass, but I do enjoy the challenge of seeing how many pieces of bacon I can consume without negative internal issues. I'd like to keep going so you really know that I'm securely entrenched in my manhood, but I should probably move on.

The reason I waste your time proving myself to you is because yesterday, while in the lobby of a hotel, I was watching a morning news show where the newscasters were sharing the story of Christian the Lion. There's a book about this lion available, so I'll spare you the details, but essentially these two dudes who lived in London decided to purchase and try raising a lion together. Even though they didn't know much about lions, they apparently did a great job. Eventually, when their pet lion reached adult size, they felt compelled to release it into the African wild. They weren't sure if he would survive, and it was incredibly painful for them to say goodbye to Christian.

A year later, they decided to return to Africa and see how the lion they had raised was doing and whether he would still recognize them. They had a video camera on the scene when Christian came out of the woods, and the news show let us watch their reunion. It was pretty amazing! Christian the Lion came slowly out of the savanna, caught wind of his old friends, and then saw them off in the distance. Excitedly, he rushed toward them and mauled them with love and licks and lion hugs and all sorts of other feline mushy stuff. As I watched, I had to look around to make sure no one was watching me, because I was whimpering like a teenage cheerleader who just got dumped by her first boyfriend.

So why all the emotion? Whenever I see someone invest time and energy and love into something and then willingly sacrifice it, giving away what they have, it's powerful!

I've seen a similar story played out many times when I've been fortunate enough to officiate weddings. Just last year in Adullam, I performed thirteen wedding ceremonies. Most of them were in beautiful settings. Some were in the Rocky Mountains, often overlooking spacious woods, canyons, or rivers. Some were in the city in ornate churches, and two were actually on beaches — one in Florida and one in Cancún.

Most of the couples I knew very well. As I had a hand in even helping some of them connect, I always felt compelled to get to know the parents during the preliminaries. On the rehearsal day, the moms were usually busy, scurrying around working, while the dads tended to lie back, grab a beer, and wait for their one and only responsibility. Although the job of the bride's father is pretty easy, I've learned that I need to have them practice it at least once. Their primary task? To give away their daughter, the bride.

Most of the fathers I've had the privilege of knowing were pretty burly dudes, hearty blokes with calloused hands, a hard work ethic, and broken-down bodies as evidence. Yet without exception I find that during the trial run these guys seem to get really quiet, sometimes even welling up with a few tears. It's only practice, but they seem to suddenly get serious when the thought hits them and they realize they are about to say goodbye to their little lady.

The next day, the real deal happens. After the procession, a few songs are sung, maybe a reading or two, then the music changes to signal the entrance of the bride. As the reverend, I always try to remain composed ... after all, that is my job. But something diabolical happens to me at this point. I always make the mistake of looking at the face of the bride's father. Most of the time you can see the dad starting to quiver, his eyes filling with moisture as he reflects on how important this girl has been to him. Most men don't think in detailed pictures, but no dad can forget the thousands of memories: the times we protected them, worked hard to provide for them, taught them to drive, took them to practice, rooted for them in the bleachers, or drove them to their first day of college. It's just too darn much to take in! Every time I see the face of that father, I just lose it and have to fight to keep from bawling like a baby.

The father slowly walks his cherished daughter down the aisle. The music stops. Dad stands proudly, painfully holding back his emotions, as I say, "Who gives this woman to be joined in marriage with this man?" After a pause, the father responds, "I do." He then takes his daughter's arm and gently unwraps it from his, bends down to kiss his baby goodbye, and extends her hand out toward this new man and her new life with him.

I realize that some people today think that marriage is old-fashioned and unrealistic. And there are people today who feel the same way about the church. They think the church is outdated, boring, worthless, archaic, self-serving, and out of touch, a waste of time and a poor use of money. But the Scriptures speak clearly for God when they call the church his bride, and it is in this title and in the essence of being given away that we will find the meaning and reason to keep going.

I share this reminder of the church because I know how easy it is to forget this amid the mundane duties often required to lead a church. So many—dare I say the majority?—of existing pastors and church planters we've run with often speak respectfully, but discouragingly, about what life has become for them serving in vocational ministry. Things like sermon preparation, staff issues, people in constant crisis, friends letting you down, constant critique from other people (and yourself), people expecting more time than you can give, your spouse and children not getting enough of your time or the right type of time, arguments over silly stuff like how we sing to God, what we should do with church money, how do we get more church money without making it seem like we want their money, how we relate to our denomination when they seem to be out of touch and unwilling to measure or manage the right things, not to mention clarifying vision, values, mission, and blah blah blah ...

I suppose you could add a few hundred of your own personal zingers. Add to these struggles the myriad internal pressures of trying to be an authentic person, a faithful leader amid peer pressure, trying to perform and succeed (or at least to save face) while fighting to live as a true missionary, and spending time with those outside the church walls when it seems as though the only way to hold "the thing" together is to spend more time in the church building.

Without a reminder of the bigger picture of God's church, we can often settle for a view of church leadership that is more like cleaning the garage or babysitting than the adventurous voyage we believe it should be. What should be the best thing in the world isn't at all compelling or curious to the unchurched. Most of the time it's not even all that meaningful for a good majority of those in the church. We know the *idea* of church still makes a lot of sense, and at times we garner more buy-in from the congregation and compel folks to get more involved or to be more committed. Yet at the end of each week, we feel as if we're still trying to lasso mice or sell sand to people who live on the beach.

So how are we to feel about *church*? How are we to feel about *God*, for that matter? Why should we continue to justify the toll it plays on our psyche and our families? Does God really expect his leaders to continue to fight through all of this without heavy doses of Prozac?

And yet, miracle of all miracles, more and more leaders keep signing up and trying to make it happen. It's sort of like watching ten well-trained bull riders get kicked off, stepped on, ground into the dirt, and gored. Yet for some strange reason the next guy happily ropes in and rides the same bull. There's just something about this thing called *church* that captures our hearts and keeps us fighting for a better day.

Maybe it's that exhilarating feeling you get when one—yes, even *one*—person moves an inch forward spiritually. Or hearing a couple say they've found a home in your church, or knowing that people took care of someone in need or bailed someone out. Twice a year we baptize people in a lake by my house, and I have never driven home from those times dry-eyed. There is nothing quite like the thrill of witnessing a whole community of people, standing ankle deep in the water, express their allegiance with scared but smiling "dunkees." It's about the best feeling in the world. Although the good moments don't seem to come as often as the difficult moments, I think I'm beginning to understand why I'm doing this church thing after all.

It's sort of like that part of the lion story where the two guys send their beloved Christian away, or where the father gives his daughter away to experience the joy of a new life with her husband. It's the *sentness* of the church—giving ourselves away so that others can know God—that keeps us all in the game, playing our hearts out. The mysterious awe associated with the Bride of Christ is in the character of her sacrificial and missional calling. The church is beautiful because it is endowed with the purpose of giving herself away wholeheartedly to the world God desires to redeem. To move past all the paralyzing church deconstruction, it may be helpful to rehear the story of the bride.

THE SENT STORY

The "giving away" of the church begins in Genesis 12. Although many scholars point out that the church was not formally born until the New Testament, all would agree that God begins the work of sending a redemptive people on mission in these early chapters of Genesis. Up to this point in the biblical story, God has had an intimate relationship with just a few families. He spends most of these years straightening out the evil of humanity. Sin enters in the world through Adam and Eve, family troubles spread with Cain and Abel, and eventually the world is filled with human sin and rebellion. When enough is enough and God can't take it anymore, he wipes the world out, redeeming a few people in the family of Noah.

Yet the evil of the human race continues, and in the story of the Tower of Babel God responds to human evil by dividing people from each other, spreading them throughout the world. After Babel, human beings are now separated — not only from God, but also from one another. Strife, war, brutality, and dissension rule the day, and God begins a master plan to redeem the world, setting in motion a cross-cultural community that will bring his blessing to this messed-up world. It's a rescue plan to save sinful humanity.

In Genesis 12:1, God says to a man named Abram, "Leave your country, your people and your father's household and go to the land I will show you." Abram (later to be called Abraham) is the start of God's plan of salvation. With these words we see the Father sending his redemptive community out into the world. God the Father is starting to give his baby away on her wedding day.

In Genesis 12:2 – 3, God continues:

> I will make you into a great nation
>   and I will bless you;
> I will make your name great,
>   and you will be a blessing.
> I will bless those who bless you,
>   and whoever curses you I will curse;
> and all the peoples on earth
>   will be blessed through you.

The people of God are being sent to live in a pagan land. Why? So they may bring the blessing of God wherever they go.

Although God's call to Abraham is a beautiful send-off, like many marriages, things don't always go so well. Before too long, Abraham's missional community is thrust into chaos again. His descendants end up living as slaves in Egypt. Again, God "gives away" his people, releasing them from the slavery of Egypt through the leadership of Moses. More than a grand escape story, God is once again moving his people into a position where his larger plan of blessing the world can continue. Moses is a good leader, and he gets the people close to accomplishing God's purposes, but he too falls short.

God, thankfully, does not give up. Though the missional community of Israel has been rebellious and unfaithful, God continues to work through them and their leaders. He calls a new leader, Joshua, who brings the people across the Jordan into the Promised Land. Joshua sends two spies to check out the walled city of Jericho, the last stronghold of the Canaanites. They wisely find refuge in the home of the harlot Rahab (so no one will notice them). After staying for some time in her home, built into the wall of the city, their cover is blown and Rahab hides them from the authorities, sending the king's envoy on a wild goose chase. As the spies escape, they make a promise to this pagan prostitute that they will protect her and her entire family from the coming destruction of the city. Just as the red blood of the sheep was spread over the doorposts during the Passover, she's instructed to let a scarlet rope hang from her window to set her apart for redemption. While the city is destroyed, Rahab and her family are saved.

The blessing of God, given to Abraham for the purpose of blessing the world, is here given to a pagan lady and her family. What is amazing about this story is that Rahab is not only engrafted into the missional community of God's people, her story will eventually become an example to Jewish believers in the formative days of the New Testament church. In the New Testament letter to the Hebrews, Rahab is held up as an example of faith. In the letter of James she is celebrated for combining her faith with deeds. The story of Rahab is yet another instance of God's mission rolling on through the Old Testament, and her life reminds us that from the days of his call to Abram, God has intentionally used his people to reach across cultural lines, saving *anyone* willing to trust him.

Although an obscure story to most of us, this Rahab commercial break is a critical reminder to the Hebrew people that the God they follow and worship isn't just *their* God. It's also a great reminder to us today in the church. Like Jonah, who doubted that God would really want to save the evil Ninevites—the enemies of Israel—we may be tempted to see God's exclusiveness with the Jews as proof that he really doesn't care that much for the pagan nations, those outside the ranks of God's people. Throughout the Old Testament, God calls the Jews to be separate from the culture in which they lived. Several times he even tells them to slaughter anyone who is not of Hebrew origin! It's natural that some might be tempted to ask, "Doesn't that mean that God wants his people to avoid contact with outsiders?" I'll admit that these passages seem to contradict the missional purposes of God. When God tells his people to destroy the Canaanites, it doesn't sound like he wants them to connect with, live among, or bless them.

To unpack this seeming contradiction we need to go back to the bigger picture of what God is trying to do. Remember the "father of the bride" story? For those of us who have children, we know that you can't just send your kids out into the world without some sort of foundation being laid. A good father knows when his little girl is ready to date, and as she matures and grows, he trusts that that someday she'll be ready to be given away in marriage. Right now, my older daughter, Alli, is fifteen. She's 5 ft. 8 in., gorgeous like me and her mother (okay, gorgeous like her mother), and soon she'll be pulling into her high school parking lot in my Jeep Wrangler. She'll be the catch of the school. We all know that boys like an attractive girl who drives a jeep.

I often watch the young vultures (teenage boys) gawking at her, and I picture the type of lads who will soon be asking her out. Given the world we live in today, I assume that just about any young man who wants to date my daughter will have spent hundreds of hours surfing easily accessible porn sites, will have learned that many girls are easy to exploit for their own sexual purposes, and will probably expect the same from my baby. Alli and I have spent quite a bit of time talking about dating. I've told her that when she's thirty-eight, I'll let her begin taking phone calls! Since that probably won't work, I figure I'll have to begin trusting her with boys this next year, although I did make sure she knows that any boy who even wants a shot at taking her out must call me to ask my permission. I'm not sure exactly what my parameters will be yet, but at the very least it will include a personal interview with me and a hand-written application with essay questions about the value of women — especially how he intends to value my women! You can be sure that I'll have on my dirty old white tank top and my twelve-gauge shotgun clearly visible for the little punk who decides to court my girl.

I think this example illustrates the tension that God was dealing with as well. His goal for the Hebrew people was that they would be a unique community, extending God's blessing to every culture. But like a teenage girl, there were times when their immaturity was so apparent that he had to pull them back and remind them of their vulnerability.

Consider God's words to his people in Ezekiel 16:1 – 15:

> The word of the LORD came to me: "Son of man, confront Jerusalem with her detestable practices and say, 'This is what the Sovereign LORD says to Jerusalem: Your ancestry and birth were in the land of the Canaanites; your father was an Amorite and your mother a Hittite. On the day you were born your cord was not cut, nor were you washed with water to make you clean, nor were you rubbed with salt or wrapped in cloths. No one looked on you with pity or had compassion enough to do any of these things for you. Rather, you were thrown out into the open field, for on the day you were born you were despised.
>
> " 'Then I passed by and saw you kicking about in your blood, and as you lay there in your blood I said to you, "Live!" I made you grow like a plant of the field. You grew up and developed and became the most beautiful of jewels. Your breasts were formed and your hair grew, you who were naked and bare.

" 'Later I passed by, and when I looked at you and saw that you were old enough for love, I spread the corner of my garment over you and covered your nakedness. I gave you my solemn oath and entered into a covenant with you, declares the Sovereign LORD, and you became mine.

" 'I bathed you with water and washed the blood from you and put ointments on you. I clothed you with an embroidered dress and put leather sandals on you. I dressed you in fine linen and covered you with costly garments. I adorned you with jewelry: I put bracelets on your arms and a necklace around your neck, and I put a ring on your nose, earrings on your ears and a beautiful crown on your head. So you were adorned with gold and silver; your clothes were of fine linen and costly fabric and embroidered cloth. Your food was fine flour, honey and olive oil. You became very beautiful and rose to be a queen. And your fame spread among the nations on account of your beauty, because the splendor I had given you made your beauty perfect, declares the Sovereign LORD.

" 'But you trusted in your beauty and used your fame to become a prostitute.' "

Here we see the loving heart of a Father, nurturing his people through adolescence and preparing them to carry his name proudly through the world.

We find a similar message in Isaiah 62, as God expresses his commitment to his people:

> For Zion's sake I will not keep silent,
>   for Jerusalem's sake I will not remain quiet,
> till her righteousness shines out like the dawn,
>   her salvation like a blazing torch.
> The nations will see your righteousness,
>   and all kings your glory;
> you will be called by a new name
>   that the mouth of the LORD will bestow.
> You will be a crown of splendor in the LORD's hand,
>   a royal diadem in the hand of your God.
> No longer will they call you Deserted,
>   or name your land Desolate.

But you will be called Hephzibah,
    and your land Beulah;
for the LORD will take delight in you,
    and your land will be married.
As a young man marries a maiden,
    so will your sons marry you;
as a bridegroom rejoices over his bride,
    so will your God rejoice over you ...
They will be called the Holy People,
    the Redeemed of the LORD;
and you will be called Sought After,
    the City No Longer Deserted. (Isa. 62:1 – 12)

In both these passages we see God's desire to care for his people, calling them out from the world. But we must also note the context: God takes pleasure in his people *so that* they will make his name and his ways renowned throughout the nations. In Exodus 19:4 – 6 we also find this combination of God's calling his people to exclusive loyalty, but given within the context of influencing the world as they bring God's blessing:

You yourselves have seen what I did to Egypt, and how I carried you on eagles' wings and brought you to myself. Now if you obey me fully and keep my covenant, then out of all nations you will be my treasured possession. Although the whole earth is mine, you will be for me a kingdom of priests and a holy nation.

Though the majority of the Old Testament focuses on God's work with the Jewish people, spaced strategically throughout are windows to God's larger redemptive plan with outsiders. Persian King Darius, Jonah and the Ninevites, and even whacko Nebuchadnezzar show us how peasants and pagan kings not only acknowledged the God of the Hebrews but actually turned to him at times.

As the saga of the Old Testament fades, there are three hundred years of uncomfortable silence for God's missional people. This gap of revelation and the lack of God's guiding voice leaves the

Hebrew nation with a tenuous skepticism about their purpose—perhaps God's national calling for them has been revoked. Maybe his anger at their adolescent-like immaturity and their failure to finish the story of redemption will leave them without a home, without a purpose—without anything. The Hebrew people remain vigilant in their traditions as they become a marginalized subculture within the dominant Roman shadow. They stay together, living out the patterns of the past, but despondency rules the land. Where is God?

Priests still make sacrifices for the people, and the people continue to pray for God's help, but their faith is faltering. Then, God does something new. The story picks up again, with a barren Jewish woman named Elizabeth. She's married to a man named Zechariah. They are old, but they've been faithfully hoping for a son, as well as for Israel's God to show up again.

JESUS THE SENT ONE

Like the first sprout of a beautiful tulip emerging from the dark, cold days of winter, God's story of blessing pokes out of the ground again. After waiting years to be selected for service in the temple burning incense, Zechariah is chosen and while serving in the temple he receives an angelic visit:

> An angel of the Lord appeared to him, standing at the right side of the altar of incense. When Zechariah saw him, he was startled and was gripped with fear. But the angel said to him: "Do not be afraid, Zechariah; your prayer has been heard. Your wife Elizabeth will bear you a son, and you are to give him the name John. He will be a joy and delight to you, and many will rejoice because of his birth, for he will be great in the sight of the Lord. He is never to take wine or other fermented drink, and he will be filled with the Holy Spirit even from birth. Many of the people of Israel will he bring back to the Lord their God. And he will go on before the Lord, in the spirit and power of Elijah, to turn the hearts of the fathers to their children and the disobedient to the wisdom of the righteous—to make ready a people prepared for the Lord." (Luke 1:11 – 17)

Elizabeth does indeed become pregnant. She expresses her hope with a word of praise, giving glory to God: "The Lord has done this for me ... In these days he has shown his favor and taken away my disgrace among the people" (Luke 1:25).

While Zechariah and Elizabeth feel the winds of hope, a young woman named Mary is also awakened from her mundane life by an angel, who startles her with these words, "Greetings, you who are highly favored! The Lord is with you" (Luke 1:28). Visits from angels are amazing enough, but add to that the fact that God has been virtually silent for three hundred years and you can begin to understand why this blessing would have been a paralyzingly beautiful thing to hear.

> Mary was greatly troubled at his words and wondered what kind of greeting this might be. But the angel said to her, "Do not be afraid, Mary, you have found favor with God. You will be with child and give birth to a son, and you are to give him the name Jesus. He will be great and will be called the Son of the Most High. The Lord God will give him the throne of his father David, and he will reign over the house of Jacob forever; his kingdom will never end." (Luke 1:29–33)

Mary is given the incredible news that God has not abandoned his people. In fact, though Mary doesn't fully understand it yet, God is about to do something no one could have anticipated. But that's not what I want to point out. What I want you to notice about both of these angelic encounters is how Mary and Zechariah respond to the news they receive from God.

Mary hears of God's favor on Elizabeth and heads to Judea to celebrate. Note how she receives this promise of God's work in the context of his promise to Abraham.

And Mary said:

> "My soul glorifies the Lord
>   and my spirit rejoices in God my Savior,
> for he has been mindful
>   of the humble state of his servant.

> From now on all generations will call me blessed,
>> for the Mighty One has done great things for me—
>> holy is his name . . .
> He has helped his servant Israel,
>> remembering to be merciful
> to Abraham and his descendants forever,
>> even as he said to our fathers." (Luke 1:42–55)

Mary naturally and easily references the original blessing God promised to the whole world through Abraham.

The same blessing is also referenced by Zechariah in his great prayer of thanks to God:

> Praise be to the Lord, the God of Israel,
>> because he has come and has redeemed his people.
> He has raised up a horn of salvation for us
>> in the house of his servant David
> (as he said through his holy prophets of long ago),
>> salvation from our enemies
>> and from the hand of all who hate us—
> to show mercy to our fathers
>> and to remember his holy covenant,
>> the oath he swore to our father Abraham:
> to rescue us from the hand of our enemies,
>> and to enable us to serve him without fear
>> in holiness and righteousness before him all our days.
>> (Luke 1:68–75)

Are you beginning to see how these stories fit together? God's plan to bless, reach, include, adopt, reclaim, and redeem has not been abandoned or forgotten. It is about to touch down in every neighborhood, village, and town.

God's plan of redemption picks up steam now. John, the son of Elizabeth and Zechariah, announces that Jesus (Mary's promised son) is the Lamb of God, the one who will eventually die so that the hearts of men and women can be cleansed and renewed and God's heavenly blessing of abundant life will once again cut through the black veil of evil, injustice, poverty, pain, and prejudice.

Jesus appears in the midst of Israel announcing God's sovereign reign over the world. He calls God's reign "the kingdom" and says that it is now at hand. But there is a twist to his message. God's heavenly rule and his deliverance are not going to come in the form of a military conquest over Rome, another exodus from slavery to a foreign nation (as many expected). The kingdom will penetrate the slavery of sin and set human hearts free to live out the life that Jesus taught and demonstrated. For the next three years, as Jesus taught and healed, demonstrating the reality of God's kingdom, God's people begin to come alive, sensing that the story is once again unfolding before their eyes. God's people are once again experiencing his blessing.

Jesus continues the "sent" ways of God. He goes to a well in Samaria to give hope to a half-breed, a spiritually illegitimate woman like Rahab, who would have never thought access to God a possibility again. He visits wedding parties, hangs out with tax collectors, ministers to a centurion's family, plays with children in the streets, and spends time on mountainsides, in caves, and in city centers where the people will listen to his teaching.

After Jesus lives and works for thirty-three years, he says to his followers in John 20:21, "As the Father has sent me, I am sending you." Hear it another way. "As the Creator of all humanity gave you a perfect world and kept giving his best, he again has sent Jesus, his very best to you. You must follow suit and continue to give your lives away."

THE SENT CHURCH

Whereas his global intentions of redemptive blessing through Abraham have probably been lost on the ears of his people, we read in Matthew 16:18, as Jesus is speaking to Peter, "And I tell you that you are Peter, and on this rock I will build my church, and the gates of Hades will not overcome it." The sent community, the missional band, has now been named "the church," and it is the church that will carry forth his original design and plan. The church is now his family of priests; the church is now his called-apart and set-apart people — living holy lives in the midst of the world and showing the world the glory of God. Read Peter's own words:

> As you come to him, the living Stone—rejected by men but chosen by God and precious to him—you also, like living stones, are being built into a spiritual house to be a holy priesthood, offering spiritual sacrifices acceptable to God through Jesus Christ. (1 Peter 2:4–6)

> But you are a chosen people, a royal priesthood, a holy nation, a people belonging to God, that you may declare the praises of him who called you out of darkness into his wonderful light. Once you were not a people, but now you are the people of God; once you had not received mercy, but now you have received mercy.

> Dear friends, I urge you, as aliens and strangers in the world, to abstain from sinful desires, which war against your soul. Live such good lives among the pagans that, though they accuse you of doing wrong they may see your good deeds and glorify God on the day he visits us. (1 Peter 2:9–12)

Do you see the cohesive story? Whether you start in Genesis and go forward or start in the final letters from Jesus' most trusted allies and work backward, the theme is sure. God has always wanted a people that would be exclusive to him—holy, set apart, distinct, and beautiful to the world he is trying to redeem. Sometimes he had to call them away from pagan influences because he was trying to protect them. He had seen what happens when you let the kids play with knives. Since he promised them through Noah that he would never kick them out of the universe again, he was essentially trying to get them through adolescence. But, let the truth be clear—they were not to be separate in the sense that many evangelicals have come to believe. He didn't like them or love them more than the cultures they were often fighting. They were not privileged like a spoiled rich kid might be. They were special, and they were called beautiful because they were to represent the nature of the triune God and make God known through their mission—a mission quickened by Christ and carried forth by his New Testament church.

Since the days of Abraham, God's people have been a mission-ary community, a people for God to "give away" to the world. And God continues that purpose in the church today. Daniel Allen, one of our Missio team leaders, once described God's people in a way that has always stuck with me. He referred to the church as God's "intimate allies," his partners in redemptive mission. The church is loved by God and given intimate access to his great pas-sion of self-sacrificing love. Because she is precious to him, she is most beautiful when she reflects his deepest love and gives herself away for the sake of the world.

In our book *The Tangible Kingdom* (affectionately referred to as "TK"), I tell the story of a painful church situation. It was an experience that not only led me to uproot my family from the city we loved, but it ripped the very *sentness* that empowers all real ministry out of my heart. I was left without passion, without a purpose, and without a desire to ever do *church* again — especially the type of church that would require self-sacrificial love for the sake of others. I settled for a regular church job that provided my family a sense of safety, but didn't really extend my life outward to the world.

At the time, it felt good to chill out and come off the field, as they say, but God would not let me just stay put. Eventually, he wooed me back into service by introducing me to a woman named Fiona. If you want the gritty details, it's in chapter 1 of the TK; but suffice it to say, meeting this waitress in Queens, New York, and seeing her attraction to the idea of God's kingdom propelled us to a new city and a new mission.

The funny thing in all of this was that we really wanted to be sent, but we had no thought of church ... either going to one or starting one. What we did have after a year was a small com-munity of people, primarily what we'd call a Starbucks crowd. Most of them were outside the normal church realm, but they had taken an interest in our story, and the visibility of our faith had attracted them to us. Some of them had come to faith in Jesus, but others were simply a part of our community, still processing through their questions about God. We met Saturday nights at our home to talk over "life and God," as we called it. On one of those evenings, during a normal conversation, a girl who had come to faith with us raised her hand and asked the big question we weren't ready to answer.

"So ... is this my church?"

I glanced over at Cheryl, who was giving me the evil eye, a clear sign that I could not at any cost say yes. I looked across the living room at Matt. His facial expression said, "I can't wait to hear your response." So on the fly, I made up this great answer: "No, we're not your church; we're your ... uh ... faith community." Even as I said it, I was thinking, "Brilliant Halter, a warm fuzzy sounding answer without any commitment! You're the man!" I thought that I had wormed my way out of the dilemma. We could go back to our comfortable, nebulous missionary-ness. But the young woman kept pushing.

"Yah, that sounds good, but I came to faith and so have some others here, so aren't we supposed to go to a church?"

Now I knew I was in trouble. The room got really quiet; my wife and Matt (my other wife) had both stopped breathing, waiting for my next response. The words that I was about to say would not only serve to inaugurate a new church in Denver, but they would forever change the way I thought about missionary life and leadership. "Actually, church is something everyone should be a part of, but it's different than being a faith community. Church happens when a group of people decide to go on mission with God together."

The understudies looked confused, so I continued, "For instance, Matt, Maren, Cheryl, and I have been on mission for you. We've given up our food for you; we give up our family time and personal interests to accommodate all of your spontaneous dropping by to talk. Half the time or more, we would really rather you stay away so we can enjoy our private time; but then we see you pull up in front of the house and we give another night up for you. We throw parties and gatherings for you and your friends all the time, and although it looks like it's all fun for us, it's a heck of a lot of work! In many ways, we've died for you; and if you want to be a part of a church, you'll have to die too. You have to give your life away."

"There, how do you like that?" I thought to myself. Surely, they won't want to do church now. But then, looking at their faces, I had this strange feeling that God was up to something. They seemed as if they were seriously thinking about whether or not they wanted to die with us. Matt quickly grabbed some Post-It note pads and asked everyone to write down names of their friends whom they knew would never go to a church, but who they thought would like the type of environment we had created for them. Our little group of twenty-five people wrote down about 110 names. We decided to simply pray for a week, and then the following week we invited them back to take the final vote. It was a vote that would essentially change their lives, a vote that God would use to help me clarify my understanding of a missional church. The rest is history, as they say. Everyone came back and unanimously told us, "We'll come and die with you; we'll let God send us."

How could I say no? Though our church, Adullam, was not officially born that night, it was on that evening that God called us out and gave us the mantra that has remained constant to this day—"Come, die, and give your life away." When Christians transfer from other churches, we still interview them to discern if they really want to come and die with us. God had waited two years for me to come back, but they weren't wasted years. In my heart and mind, the question of "church" and why it existed was now answered. Church is God's people intentionally committing to die together so that others can find his kingdom. Just as God had given away his Son, he was now asking me to give my life away. In my life and the life of our new church, the bride was once again being given away—sent out into the world. It was beautiful.

Whenever I share this story with church leaders of every form, I tend to see the same look. Something about the "dying" part seems to grab everyone by the throat (like the Christian the Lion story). I've come to see that many leaders still need to learn the true meaning of church. I've heard hundreds of leaders, many of whom have large churches, say, "Been there, done that, built a church, have lots of people ... But there's got to be more." To those who now ponder the vision of starting a new church, I hear the same thing. "I just don't want to start the same ol' thing that draws a bunch of Christians from other churches. There's got to be more."

There is more!

But the things we all want to see happen will never happen until we first settle this issue of why the church exists. God's church is a *missional* church, a community that is sent and given away for God's purposes. While I believe the unsent church is still God's church, she is a bride that has lost much of her intrigue and beauty. For God's church to reemerge in your local church, you must be willing to let the bride become beautifully sent. You must allow God to send you, to send your people, and you must begin to see yourself as part of a larger story of God's mission, which began with Abram and continues today through leaders who desire to see God's marvelous ways change the course of history.

My daughter, Alli, has just turned fifteen. She got her driver's permit the day after her birthday. I had let her drive carefully up and down our street a few times prior to her birthday (don't do that, it's illegal), but eventually the day came for her to get on the real road. As we carefully pulled out of the driveway, she asked me, "Dad, can we stay on the side roads and then maybe next month try the freeway?" I'm not sure what came over me at that moment, but I turned to her and said, "Nope. We're going to go big or go home. We're taking the fast road." I glanced over at her and saw some fear in her eyes. She gripped the wheel hard with both hands. I remember seeing her forearm muscles flex and strain. She adjusted her rearview mirror, took a deep breath, and after a few seconds, she smiled.

I believe that God's people want to go BIG! They're tired of being the unsent church—weary of church services, sermons, in-house programs, and Bible studies that never push them out and challenge them to really be the missional people God has called them to be. I won't deny that it's more comfortable driving on the side roads, but after awhile they can get pretty boring. I think it's time for the church of God, in all its diverse forms, to *be* the church, to get out on the open road, and to let God smile on us as we follow him out on the highways of this world.

Let's start living out the AND and be the gathered community of God's people, sent out into the world.

CHAPTER 2

Starting the AND ...
Wherever You Are

IMAGINE THAT GOD CALLED YOU and fifteen friends to start a church in a city where you had no prior relationships and where you knew the culture at large had grown weary of religion of all types, especially those representing Christendom. Maybe it's a city like London or Amsterdam, perhaps Portland or even Denver. Your team is now living within a five-mile radius of each other in the middle of the city, and you are having your first team meeting to discuss how to give birth to a new church in this city.

What would you talk about? What would your strategy be? Imagine you have one teammate who says, "Okay, I've got a plan. Let's rent one of the old churches that's out of business and we'll put together some great flyers and kick off a really cool service in six weeks. I'll do some alternative worship experiences and someone else can prepare a great message without that entire churchy lingo. Let's also do something fun for the kids. What do you all think?"

From across the table, someone else says, "Well, isn't that what most people have done in the past? In fact, it seems like there've been two or three church plants in our neighborhood that have tried just that in the last few years, and I don't think any of them are still around. I'd hate to assume that we'd be that much different." Everyone sighs and reluctantly shoots the idea down. There's an awkward silence and the whole team sits there staring into their coffee mugs.

Finally, someone breaks the silence and says, "Why don't we take a week to study how Jesus started the church? We can all read the Gospels and then come back with some ideas."

As the team leader, you take this opportunity to buy yourself some time and save face. "Yah, great idea. We'll see ya next week."

Next week arrives and you're back at the coffee shop. "So, what did you all pick up from your reading?"

One says, "Okay, I noticed that Jesus did a lot of teaching, healing, and other impressive acts, and it drew a lot of attention, so people followed him."

Quickly, a sarcastic response returns, "Oh, that's encouraging to find out. Let's just start doing miracles!"

Another says, "I saw that Jesus spent a lot of time at people's homes, at parties, and hanging out in well-known public places."

And another says, "It seems obvious that Jesus spent time away from the crowds, spending time with a few leaders, and other times he was just praying."

Yet another speaks up, "Interestingly, he still spent time in the churches or synagogues, trying to change people's minds about what true religion was."

As the leader, you feel some tension as you try to pull everyone together. Certainly, if you isolated any one of these aspects, you could form a pretty strong argument for starting a church with almost any focus or strategy.

The last comment that is shared comes from your least mature person. She slowly raises her hand and says, "I'm not sure if this really means anything, and I don't know much about the Bible, but I tried to find Scripture where Jesus was talking about how to start a church or grow a church. I thought that if church is so important, there ought to be more info on it in the Bible. But I couldn't find anything specific at all. I read all four gospels and the only time Jesus even mentions the church is when he's talking to Peter about his leadership. I know that doesn't really help, but I thought it was interesting that in all of his ministry, teaching, and preaching Jesus never really talks about the church. All he talked about was the kingdom—it seems like his crowd just kind of grew on its own. Oh ... and I had one more thought, or actually a question. Why do you think Jesus lived like a normal person for thirty years before he even got intentional about drawing a crowd? Maybe there's something to this part of the story we don't talk much about. Jesus doesn't really seem like much of a church planter to me. He seems more like ... I don't know ..."

"A missionary," someone excitedly completes her thought.

"Hmmm," you think to yourself. "Jesus the missionary. Now that's an interesting thought. Why don't we consider a strategy based more around missionary activities than about creating church activity?"

We play with this scenario quite a bit with leaders because the only way to move toward the AND is to begin to think and act like a missionary.

Missional isn't a *form* of church. It's a label we give to the qualitative or descriptive aspect of how a church actually lives. It's about how much like Jesus those people become and how much they influence, woo, and transform the culture in which they are placed. In other words, how "missional" you are is largely determined by the extent to which your people model the life, activities, and words of Jesus. It doesn't matter how big or small your church is. Any church of any size can be both missional and nonmissional at the same time. The difference is in the lifestyle of the believers. This basic understanding of *missional* levels the playing field for us and sets up a new expectation of faithfulness for anyone who has "been there, done that" in ministry.

As Matt and I have worked across a wide variety of denominations and with thousands of church leaders, I can say with a clear conscience that the reason *all* of our church forms fail to produce the fruit we see in Scripture is because we approach church as everything *but* a missionary community. Some try to lead church as a pastor, some lead as a denominational leader, and some approach church from the angle of an evangelist, a scholar, a teacher, or CEO. Although these positions can work for a while and do have a vested interest in producing actual results, they tend to manage and measure the wrong things. If our understanding of church is not in line with our missionary calling as the people of God, the results will almost always reflect a certain amount of dissonance. We have to start (or restart) where a missionary would start; we need to begin from scratch.

EX NIHILO AND EX ECCLESIA

In seminary, I learned a term that has for some strange reason always stuck with me. The term is *ex nihilo*, which is translated "out of nothing." We've often used this as the tagline for our missionary church plant processes since it denotes the idea of starting from scratch, *nada*, zippo — nothing.

We talk about church planting this way: "Creating church where it doesn't exist."

The missionary flow that we're talking about begins with nothing. Many people have started churches by hiving off a subset of existing Christians from another church, or gathering disconnected believers from around a city. This is all well-intentioned and probably better than nothing, but we've found that in most cases these groups are still starting a church with a church. They may have a few months of core group gatherings, but in most cases, a church service eventually begins and the church is perceived to have "launched."

We've coached many people who have followed this approach and invariably they don't follow a basic missionary flow. So let's begin by looking at how a missionary team (that is, any band of concerned Christians sent on mission for God) *should* behave. What exactly is a basic missionary flow? If you're reading this from the standpoint of an existing church, don't tune out or flip ahead. The AND of missional/incarnational ministry can begin in churches of any form — even if they emerge *ex ecclesia* (you should be able to figure this out). Your job will be just a bit different, starting the missionary flow from your existing structures, so stick around! We'll address your specific issues in a few pages.

Starting from scratch

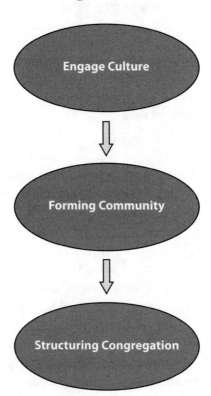

ENGAGE CULTURE

The first phase of any mission must involve *cultural engagement*. Engagement of culture may *sound* like evangelism, but it's really about "context." Context is a basic missionary concept anyone learns before beginning *ex nihilo*. It's best understood by looking at the negative definition of "taking something out of context." We all know what this means. It involves misusing information, exploiting one side of a story for one's personal agenda, or naïve handling of an idea. The word itself means, "the whole situation, background, or environment relevant to some happening or personality." One of the words it's derived from is *com-texture,* which means "to weave."

Pulling all of this together, we can say that *context* is the background understanding that God has been at work weaving together Spirit-led thoughts, dreams, and kingdom innovations in a city, in a neighborhood, and in the life of every person you'll meet. Context should stop you in your tracks on a regular basis and propel you to find out every little detail you can about a person, avoiding assumptions or preconceived notions about what they want or are looking for.

Context is one of those words that most people understand conceptually but rarely take as seriously as they should in real life. We do demographic studies to get context; we talk to other pastors in the area we are trying to reach to find out what they've experienced; we read books about the makeup of generational thinking, societal trends, and personal worldviews; but we rarely do what a *missionary* must do to really know the context from which a church can emerge. So how does a missionary get the context? We do it by becoming friends with people.

Why is becoming friends so important? Why can't we just take a few months and survey people as they come in and out of their local grocery store? Think about your normal relationships with your spouse, your closest friends, or your own children. Isn't it true that the more you get to know someone, the more you are able to relate with him or her the way you should? For instance, Matt has been my ministry partner for the last six years. We've probably spent more time together than we care to admit. We've enjoyed the same recreational activities, we started Adullam and Missio together, we facilitate an online training program called Missional Church Apprenticeship Practicum (MCAP) together, and we live a few minutes apart. I can honestly say that, outside of our spouses, we probably know each other's way of thinking, emotional reactions, and general way of being in almost any situation.

Those who don't know us very well generally perceive me to be the winsome, relational guy, while Matt always gets tagged as the elusive, quiet fellow. Over the course of our ministry together, I have had a number of people say, "Man, it's hard to read Matt." He seems intimidating and a tad unapproachable. I always smile when I hear that because Matt has said that I often get the same label from people who know him better. Some people love me, and some people think I'm as nasty as a junkyard dog. Some people feel Matt is like a wise father, and some would just as soon run him over with a dull-bladed rototiller because he's spoken truth in ways they don't like.

Here's a reality check. Context takes *time* to develop and unpack. And that's why you must learn to engage the culture with the primary motivation of becoming friends, weaving a web of relationships across a region of your city.

This is also a good time to take a look at the idea of being *incarnational*. As we've talked about earlier, being *missional* is about our *sentness*—it represents the directional impulse of every church and every Christian into the world. Being *incarnational* is not so much about our direction; it's more about *how* we go, *what* we do as we go, and how we are postured in the culture God calls us to engage. Incarnation is the personality of our proclamation.

One of the most profound things about Jesus (which is often overlooked) is that he hung around for thirty years without planting a church or starting a small group. He was just there living a regular life. Though he was labeled a friend of sinners during his formal period of ministry for hanging out with certain groups of people, the truth is that Jesus spent his entire life becoming friends with sinners. He knew his context by name and face.

When Matt and I moved our families to Denver, we had a goal of becoming friends with about fifty people. We also qualitatively measured being a friend by how many of them invited us to be with their friends. We didn't have a church to invite people, nor were we even sure we would be leading a church. All we knew is that God was calling us to be missionaries, and we set out to make it happen. We threw parties all the time, often had people over to our home, made the most of spontaneous times, and tried to become the life of our neighborhood and any place where relationships were being forged.

As we engaged the culture as missionaries, our "street cred" increased; we became the "go to" people when an emergency happened, and people expected us to initiate a lot of great times together. After about twelve months, we had become really good friends with about as many people as we set out to know. When we threw a party, there were always around fifty people jammed in our house. When we finally invited people to an informal Easter brunch, we had about 125 folks join us.

For anyone who wishes to see a substantive level of relational and spiritual movement, the place to begin is by engaging the culture. But as you can tell from our story, it only happens over time. Let's stop for a moment and go back to the scenario we envisioned at the start of this chapter. You are leading a church planting team in a large city like London. How long do you think it would take each of your core team members to become good friends with five to ten people? One month, maybe two? I've asked this question all over the world, literally, and everyone comes back with approximately the same time: *two years!* No matter where you live in the world, people intuitively know that friendships and "street-cred" take time, and there seems to be a general rule that a couple years are needed before you'll belong with people and they'll belong with you.

Sadly, most church plant funding models provide too much up-front funding and then phase it out to nothing just about the time a good new church pioneer has gotten his or her legs about them as a missionary. As well, if I as a consultant suggested that any new functional outreach program of a church would take two years just to get some spiritual inertia, I doubt many pastors would do the hard work or be patient enough with their people. We just seem to always want a quick fix. There's no easy way to say this. The negative or disinterested perception of the church by those outside will not change quickly. Although we can spruce things up on the inside to keep those on the inside happy, we'll see no substantial change in the culture until our collective personality, posture, and positioning changes. We have to be patient as any good missionary community would be.

Without a friendship-level understanding of people, we tend to make coarse generalizations, false assumptions, and judgmental

analyses, and we initiate arrogant movement toward people. We
fail the context test. Engaging culture isn't as much about doing
evangelism as it is incarnating the presence of Christ in every relationship we form. If we fail at engaging well and living as Christ
would live among our neighbors and friends, we fail as missionaries and the culture doesn't see the visible beauty of the sent church.

FORMATION OF BIBLICAL COMMUNITY

The second part of the missionary flow is what we call *community
formation*. This is the natural second phase of life as a missionary,
not because it's a "step" but because it's all you can really do when
you start everything from scratch.

Imagine that your mission's community does a great job with
cultural engagement. Let's say after the first round of strategy sessions twelve to twenty-four months ago, all your people incarnate
well into their communities. Some get jobs in retail stores, some
work in coffee shops, some in restaurants, some in flower shops,
schools, and government positions. If each of them becomes friends
with even a handful of people and they begin growing in their
spiritual curiosity and their relational connection to you, what do
you think the natural next step will be? Invite them to church?
Well, at this point you don't have one (at least by name), so that
option is out. What you have at this point is a faith community.

For us, we didn't have a church service or a large spiritual gathering to which to invite them, nor would it have been an appropriate
option at this point. Instead, we began to formulate and define the
essence of an intentional community. As people moved toward us
in friendship, they noticed that we had *other* things we did together
as a community. Through ad hoc discussions about God and the
way we lived our lives, and then later as they participated with us in
benevolent action and observed us participating in spiritual times
together around Scripture or Christian holidays, they knew there
was something more to our identity. None of them would have
called us a church (and we didn't use that term ourselves), but they
often asked us things like, "So what are you guys really all about?"

As we began to connect our friends together socially and recreationally, they began to invite themselves into our spiritual community. One couple actually asked me one day, "So Hugh, why were all the cars out in front of your house the other night?"

"Oh, that's just Matt and Maren, and Rich and Laura, and a few others you know. About every week or two, we like to have some time together where we intentionally talk about life and God."

"Is that something that is open for us to come to?"

"Sure, whenever you want. From now on, I'll let you know when we're getting together."

This has been a pretty consistent description of the "flow" of how people have moved toward us, and we feel that missionary communities can and should experience this same process anywhere. You may have noticed that a key to success in this flow is to avoid letting the two processes become isolated from each other. In missionary flow, these two functions constantly serve each other and allow for God to move people together and toward a common spiritual center—toward Christ. As our community begins to form, we are also continuing to engage more people.

The other critical element that really sets the process apart from the standard weekly church service rhythm is that the formation of community precedes any discussion or look of *church*. If you're from the organic/house church camp, your definition of church will give you permission to call it church, but you may not want to, at least publicly. Yes, you're creating church, or what we would call the substructure of church. But, if you're truly intending to reach the unchurched, you're not going to be able to get them to "do" church in any form, be it house church, megachurch, or whatever church. If you live in a Western context that is recovering from Christendom, people will sniff out "churchyness" and opt out. But they often feel compelled to participate and move seamlessly into spiritual community as long as it doesn't appear to have false motives or a predetermined structure.

It's a pretty safe generalization to say that "contextually," people are leery of organized anything or institutional anything, especially church. Yet they are still intuitively drawn to authentic environments where they can find friends and grow as persons, even if they are spiritual environments. This is why the formation of incarnational community is critical in a missionary context.

WHAT'S HAPPENING DURING THESE TWO PHASES?

Before we move to the final aspect of missionary flow, it may help to identify some of the key things you should focus on during the first two phases.

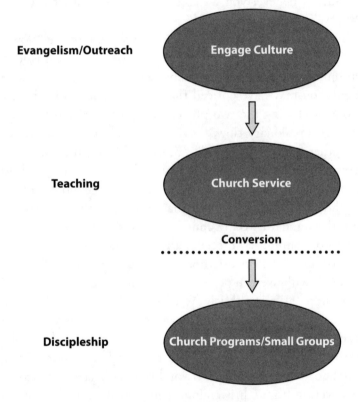

Evangelism/Outreach   Engage Culture

Teaching   Church Service

Conversion

Discipleship   Church Programs/Small Groups

Traditional Ministry Flow

To give some clarity, we show here the basic ministry flow of many attractional or traditional types of churches. You'll notice that it reflects a process where evangelism efforts, or *outreach*, are considered to be the first steps; getting them to a church service is the second step, and discipleship begins just after conversion. In other words, we have continued to perceive discipleship as something you do after someone has come to Christ and is brought into church.

Because of this, we tend to do discipleship from within the church context and generally only with people who have *come* to us. Teaching is reserved for people have *come* into the church, and any sort of deeper life discipleship, raised to the level of apprenticeship where a person is *sent* out into the world (like a missionary), is left out. I believe we lower the bar of expectations when it comes to discipleship because the evidence before our eyes seems to scream that we don't really have much hope of getting people further than a cognitive buy-in, change of belief system, and church attendance.

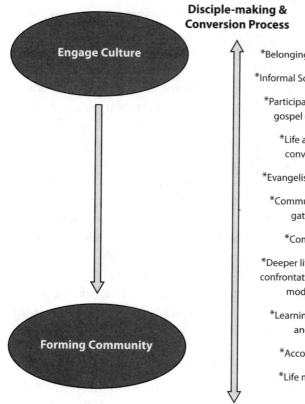

**Disciple-making &
Conversion Process**

*Belonging environments

*Informal Scripture teaching

*Participation in holistic
gospel experiences

*Life application
conversations

*Evangelistic movement

*Communal spiritual
gatherings

*Communion

*Deeper life application/
confrontation/behavioral
modification

*Learning to give $$
and time

*Accountability

*Life mentoring

Engage Culture

Forming Community

Missionary Flow

As you look at the missionary flow side, you'll see a systemically different picture. The most marked difference may be that missionaries start the discipleship process much sooner. Whenever I meet someone and we become friends, I internally believe that I'm now in a relationship where they are going to be watching my life, picking up on my values, and giving me opportunities to encourage them toward my way of life. In other words, early in the engaging culture process, discipleship and conversion begin.

When Jesus called the first disciples and actually began his discipleship process, they weren't exactly going to church as we commonly conceive it. The discipleship of Jesus was more about his walking with them in real life, talking to them about a new life, and showing them a better way to live—a more truthful truth, a nonreligious way to love God. Their process of conversion was simultaneous to their process of discipleship.

Trust me, if your community engages well and makes authentic friendships with people, and if those people begin to fuse into the spiritual hunger of your community, you will be end up doing *outside* a church context exactly what you've been sitting around in the pews waiting to do *inside* a church context. You'll be a witness through your life and words. You'll be modeling Christlike behavior; you'll be mentoring on life skills and kingdom living; you'll be teaching Scripture, confronting sin, encouraging faith, and shepherding; and in turn, disciples will be made. Most important, before someone even has to struggle with what the church is and what their responsibility is as a part of the church, they'll already know what it means to be a part of the church.

Again, those of you in the organic/house church movement will say, "Great, we're just building the church and we'll just keep doing this." Regardless, you'll still have to move to the third sphere of missionary life. Let me explain.

STRUCTURING CONGREGATION

This final phase isn't the final phase because it means you're done. It simply represents the reality that everyone who follows the first two phases of missionary flow will eventually have to figure out:

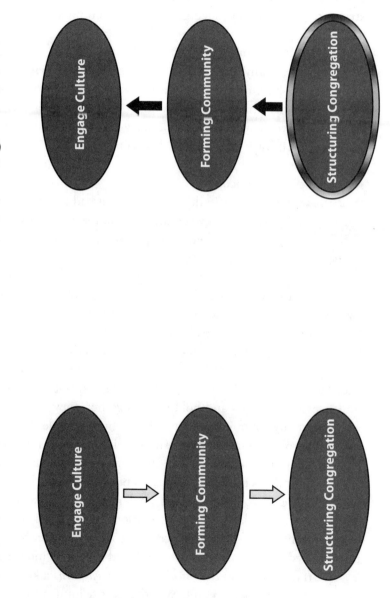

Starting from structure

Engage Culture ← Forming Community ← Structuring Congregation

Starting from scratch

Engage Culture → Forming Community → Structuring Congregation

how to hold people together in mission! It doesn't matter what your definition of church is as long as you realize that if disciples continue to be made, you're going to have to provide at least some structure for their continued growth, connection, and common vision.

The MCAP training environment that Matt and I facilitate tends to draw many leaders who are passionate for their friends while at the same time ardently afraid of organized structures. We have learned that if someone doesn't have a plan for success, they simply won't succeed. The old adage is true, "If you aim at nothing you'll hit it every time." Everyone loves the way *engaging culture* sounds. It gives the impression of fun and meaningful relational time with people.

Formation of community doesn't sound that bad either, but anyone who has tried to hold even a small group together knows that it can be pretty tough. Whether we are formally training leaders in the MCAP or informally training them in Adullam, we coach our church planters and high level leaders toward a twelve- to sixteen-month metric of developing a community of approximately twenty-five to forty people. At least one third of this group should be comprised of people outside of church, and as a leader they are beginning to hold at least two communities together.

Why do we establish these measurements? To put it bluntly, if a leader or "church planter" doesn't have the capacity to develop multiple communities and hold them together, they may not be wholeheartedly committed to pastoring a church. If a leader hasn't thought through what happens after the living room is full, they aren't likely to fill the living room in the first place. Their lack of vision will limit their intentionality and persistence and the results will be another myopically focused small group. This is why Matt and I refer to Adullam as a "congregational network of incarnational communities." We want to create a cohesive balance between the scattered communities and the gathered corporate movement.

The transition from *community* to *congregation* is a key developmental and maturing point. Whether it is helping a jaded past churchgoer reform and reengage the power of the corporate, congregational calling, or helping a new disciple understand their life in context of a greater movement, we must inspire people to think beyond their living room.

All leaders must intentionally provide a structure that will continue to both *gather* AND *scatter* God's people for mission. Matt will unpack the AND of these two primary functions of church later, but for now, it's important to note that churches of any and every form must have an intentional missional flow.

STARTING THE FLOW OF MISSION FROM ANYWHERE

I know what many of you are thinking at this point: "Yah Halter, I wish I could just start over with such a clean missionary flow, but I'm slammed! I lead one of these structured churches right now and our corporate paradigm is pretty nonmissional. In fact, our structure calcified into a hard lump of coal ten years ago. Is there any way for us to be this stuck AND move toward missional ways of church?"

The quick answer is yes. To get your people living as missionary bands engaging culture with the fervor you believe they should is simply a matter of discipleship. It is not just possible; it should be fought for and prayed into at least a percentage of every church. Will you be able to get everyone on mission? Of course not. There will always be people who love the Lord, love the church, and continue to live a faithful life under the old context. For these, we suggest giving them the grace to stay and hope that the missionary ways rub off on them. Encourage their support for those who are leading the way forward, but don't get frustrated that not everyone dances in unison to the new beat.

Practically, the answer to "Is it possible to change a church toward mission?" is to simply go backward. In other words, begin the missionary flow from your existing structure. Let's color in the lines.

GOING BACKWARD TO GO FORWARD

Just about every leader wants to "engage culture." We want our churches to live missionally, and we want our people to learn that they can live a larger gospel experience than they have been. On

many occasions, we have all preached a message or set up programs that we thought would move people out to engage their
neighbors. And we all know the typical results. Our people
think to themselves, "Oh, there goes the Rev. trying to fire us up
again to do friendship evangelism so we can invite them back to
church." These types of approaches will probably not sustain a
missionary context.

There's a bigger issue at play here than just getting people to
go and hang out with people outside the church. The core issue
is a missionary question: "How can we best engage the culture to
which God has called us?" In our present context, we believe the
answer we are suggesting in this book closely mirrors the missionary context of the early church. The community, not the individual, is the primary witness to this "bigger" gospel.

Whether you're starting from scratch and moving down the
missional flow or starting from an existing structure and moving
up, you'll notice that the center of the process is "incarnational
community." We have given an entire book to this concept (*The
Tangible Kingdom*), as well as created an eight-week incarnational
community training guide (*The TK Primer* [Anaheim, CA: CRM
Empowering Leaders, 2009]), because we believe this central concept ties good missionary engagement to the concept and reality of
the church as the missions community. If you haven't familiarized
yourself with our idea of incarnational community, essentially it's
a substructure of church where a small band of "missional people"
intentionally integrate into the lives of the unchurched.

If you want your existing church to successfully engage the
culture, you don't begin by telling your people to engage and then
bring 'em to church. You must start by creating a new environment for them that provides a better witness to the culture and is
the best way to see the kingdom lived out in concrete ways. The
incarnational community that forms can then go out together and
will eventually form the bridge between your cultural engagement
with the world and the corporate structure of the church.

While a pure, start-from-scratch mission typically begins with
engagement, then forms into community, and eventually morphs

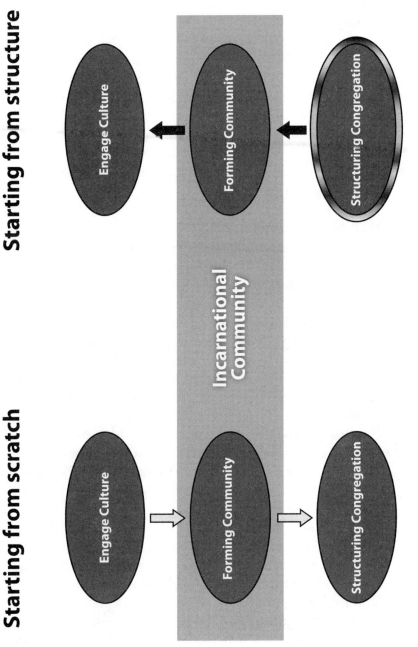

Starting from structure

Engage Culture

Forming Community

Structuring Congregation

Incarnational Community

Starting from scratch

Engage Culture

Forming Community

Structuring Congregation

into congregational structures, an existing church must first gather bands of missional people out of the larger body, bring them together, and then begin the process of engagement. All you need is a handful of people who want to pilot an incarnational community. You don't have to hit an iceberg and capsize the whole ship; you just have to send out a few people by cover of night to begin the new voyage. Will one little schooner change the direction of the ship? Not by itself. But eventually the stories of the missional communities will filter up into the general church population and begin perking curiosity and stirring up more buy-in for the next wave of would-be missionaries and missionary communities.

THE BRILLIANCE OF PILOTS

We all need a process of change. As leaders, we get months, sometimes years, to process new theories we are hearing about and think through all the missional books we're reading. Why don't we give our parishioners the same luxury? Consider starting some reading groups. Have them read Reggie McNeal's *The Present Future* or our *The Tangible Kingdom*. They're both "relatively" sensitive to the struggle many will have, but they can lead the open-minded forward. When they're done, invite the most interested to consider a pilot community who will take twelve months to explore missional/incarnational ways of living.

We recommend using the concept of a "pilot" because it takes the pressure off you as the leader and those trying a new way. If the project fails, it's actually no failure. It's simply "R & D" (Research and Development), and everyone knows in times of perceived change, it's always prudent to try new things. Whenever Matt and I work with existing congregations, we now encourage this two-part entrance into missional church (thought-leadership reading groups and pilot communities). And in the meantime, we downplay any corporate talk. This should be a stealth movement, and you can keep your existing structures unchanged ... at least for a while.

All real change happens at the grass roots level, and as people find their stride, they will naturally want to help others find the new way. All a leader has to do is sanction the process and give quiet permission to a small pilot community. In most cases, we suggest that pastors consider sensitively and relationally recruiting 10 percent of their congregation for the quiet initiative of incarnational community. If you pastor a church of three hundred, you may think, "Why would I put that much time into thirty people?" The simple answer is that even if you can see good missionary movement with only that 10 percent, they will usually outpace what your whole church does in a given year.

Another benefit of "tithing" your people back to mission is that as you release them from all duties inside the church walls, you'll be recruiting new people to cover the work they did inside the church. It will help you to develop those who are on the sidelines and encourage them to take new steps of discipleship as well. Even if the smaller bands you develop don't end up saving the world, you and your leaders will still be blessed to learn and grow together.

SHEPHERDING THE "SENDING" FROM INSIDE THE STRUCTURE

A dear friend of mine named Gary has been asked to start a new congregation within a multisite congregational structure. Gary is one of our Missio guys in Canada, and he "gets it" as much as anyone I know. But he also felt a strange call to try to model incarnational church while linking arms with a more traditional congregation. He shared these words with me in an email he titled "Turning Rocks into Gems," after meeting with a large group of Christians from this mega-church who were thinking about joining his new congregation:

> Hugh, I agree with Daniel Allen who shared his story in your MCAP training that selling the Missional Church principles to long term churchland folks is like selling rocks in a gravel quarry. At the beginning you tend to get a lot of strange looks. This is how it has been for me for the last 8 months as I've tried to encourage a new path among a very faithful core of believers

who have come from more attractional paths. I was starting to think it will not work, and I hear the warnings from many of my other friends who say [things like] "get out now, don't wait, you're dreaming, tell me of a hybrid story that works, there is no story because it will not work." Really, I am not a patient man, but I do think patience is a key fruit of the Spirit one needs in order to sell missional church rocks. Eight months of patience is an eternity for a guy like me, and I was almost ready to get out before it was too late. But last night at our gathering a shift happened — ROCKS BECAME GEMS. The penny dropped, many swallowed the missional pill, and they drank the Kool-Aid. The look in many of their eyes at what they were seeing as rocks worth nothing became priceless Kingdom Gems. Let me just list a few of the comments (Gems) that were shared openly to all at the close of the evening.

"This is all about being a community to add value to our city."

"This building we have is not mainly for worship gatherings, but to be used to bless the outside community; let's open the doors."

"I need to live as salt and light so as to add value and blessing to my street, to my neighborhood, so that if my family were to move, the street would miss us and grieve when we left."

"It's the call for all of us to live out the gospel."

"Missional Church changes everything."

Hugh, you may be used to this kind of talk, but the week before I was getting comments like, "Will we have Pastor Mark from the main campus on video" or "I hope we have good black and white Bible teaching." But now I see that a change of heart can happen, and just maybe a change of life will follow.

—Gary Swabe

Gary models something that most leaders miss. He's willing to "shepherd" people into the change instead of forcing it on them. You may be wondering, "Do you really think that everyone, given enough time, will buy the rocks?" No, I don't, but I do believe many more will buy them than won't if they are given enough time to consider a new way of church.

Does everyone have the patience needed to do this? No. And if that's you, then you are probably better off just starting from pure scratch. Yet I know that many of you still feel an incredible love for God's existing church. You know the people in these churches are true blue in their devotion to God and the Scriptures, and they have been faithfully supporting the nonmissional mission of the church forever. You feel that a good heart without missionary knowledge is easier to work with than starting with someone who doesn't yet know God.

If that describes you, then hang in there! There are still hundreds of thousands of entrenched believers who sense the winds of change coming, but they just want a little time to process before they jump in and abandon everything that has been truly meaningful to them. Learn from the mistakes of the purists. Don't just announce one day that you're changing the church. Instead, begin a faithful process of piloting missional, incarnational communities within your existing church structure.

To summarize what we're saying in this chapter, we are calling the church, in any and every form and at any stage of development, to create missionary structures and to develop momentum for incarnational community. We've suggested that you use wisdom and work quietly, creating grassroots inertia while still holding the less missional people together. At some point you will likely run into people who will challenge the missionality of your church and the sensitive changes you've made, but we believe that the process can be much less tension-filled than it has to be as long as you start by piloting. People rarely desire full-scale change, but those who love Christ and are open to the call of his missional adventure will be willing to try a more intentional way of following Jesus. As their leaders, you must provide this way for them.

CHAPTER 3

Consumerless Church: Every Church's Dream, Every Church's Nightmare

It's 4:00 a.m. I've fallen asleep on the couch in our family room and never made it up to our bedroom. I'm awakened by a strange noise that has been tormenting me all night. It's a rhythmic sound that goes for two to three seconds and then stops, then after another five to seven seconds begins again. I stare at the ceiling trying to hear where it's coming from and get a better sense if it might be an intruder or ... I don't know. I've never heard anything like it before.

I finally get up and follow the noise to our laundry room. After flicking on the light switch, the noise leads me to look down into our turtle's cage on the floor. I look to see if Tdog, as I call him, might be trying to climb up his cage, but he's just chillin' and eating some lettuce. Then suddenly, right above my head, I hear the noise again! Startled, I jump back and notice a new animal that has apparently been added to our family. (This is not surprising. Ever since my girls both hit adolescence, no one asks permission from me anymore.) It's some type of rodent, most likely a hamster or a rat, and he's running on one of those rodent wheels.

As I watch him running along, I am surprised at how fast the little guy is going. But even more than his speed, I am struck by how focused and persistent he is. He runs really fast and then he puts on the brakes. Then he starts up again, all the while just staring ahead at the wheel in front of him. After watching him for ten minutes or so, it dawns on me that I have been listening to him all night. He has been running all night, going nowhere — the constant rhythm, exertion, and short blips of breathing — but still the same mundane activity over and over again in the dark!

My hope for this book is that it will push the church, in all forms, to find God's balance: gathering people well AND missionally scattering them as incarnational communities. One of our goals is to convince you that every church and church leader is better off when they take both sides of this equation seriously. As you read, you may find yourself wanting to ask process questions like, "How do I add ___ to my service? How do I do more ____? How do I reprioritize around these new habits?"

But let me warn you up front. This chapter is really about *not* doing something. It's intended to challenge each of us to work *against* that same sinister cycle of activity that drives our churches and rarely produces anything that is good and lasting. This cycle of meaningless activity is something that happens naturally when leaders lose sight of the main thing. Instead of being driven by the missional purpose of the church, something else has us all running and getting sweaty, but not getting much further down the road. Do you know what it is?

It's consumerism.

Consumerism is the self-focused drive to get as much as I can get with the least amount of effort. It coercively shifts the church away from its true call, from valuing giving to getting. It compels us to protect what we already have and only to give away what has become useless to us. It erodes our sense of duty, honor, loyalty, and chivalry to live for the right things and the best things. It gets in the way of leaving a legacy for those behind us because it waters down our present understanding of what it means to follow Christ today. It pushes responsibility and expectations onto others instead of self and exchanges true spiritual growth for ankle-deep personal devotionals and self-help measures.

Consumerism only exists when it is *allowed* to exist. Like a scavenging raven, it only shows up where the easy food is available. Consumerism can only exist if there's something to be consumed. In American "Churchland," both spiritual leaders who provide the goods and those who consume the goods are to blame. In a sense, they are eating each other and producing little kingdom fruit. Once the goods are provided, and they continue to be delivered in the same fashion over and over by the same providers, humans naturally start to devalue what was once a deeply desired commodity. In a sense, they give ownership and responsibility to whoever provides for them. They stop growing on their own and no longer dream about the plans God might have for their lives. Hearts that were once growing and alive begin to atrophy; leaders grow weary, and the church shrivels—in numbers *and* depth of spiritual maturity.

DO I HAVE TO STAY ON THE WHEEL?

Like Satan with his offer of an apple, the consumeristic wheel subverts a leader's natural and healthy willingness to lead God's people into:

- ⇨ feeling duty-bound to provide a safe, well-staffed place for great worship and programs that minister to all the congregation's felt needs.
- ⇨ feeling responsible for crisis management and counseling, social services, administration, and spiritual formation.
- ⇨ feeling pressure to provide outlets for the artistically or musically oriented to live out their passions by producing drama or social entertainment environments.

⇨ feeling compelled to organize gathering spots for groups in the community like polling stations, coffee shops, children's school, fitness centers, and religious training.

Have you fallen into the consumerist trap? Yes, it's a trap, because we often feel that if we don't do all these things, the next hard-working, well-funded leader will, and our folks will trade us in for the newer, upgraded church experience! We'd love to get off this consumer Habitrail wheel, but that would mean an unsure future. Every sized church deals with this struggle. Even when our church, Adullam, was twenty people jammed in my house, I still lay awake at night wondering how to keep people with us.

There's at least one good thing about acknowledging our rodentlike existence: it should eventually force you to ask the right questions. The pain of providing what people *want* instead of what they *need* will eventually either kill you or cause you to ask, "Why am I doing this anyway? Is this worth all the agony? What was the Main Thing I'm trying to do again?"

It's time for us to stop spinning plates to keep people happy and entertained. As leaders, we must clarify what we're called to do and how we're called to lead, and get back to the Main Thing! Each church has a unique thumbprint given specifically by God, but every church must also answer the larger call for which we will *all* someday have to give an account.

I realize that you may have spent thousands of dollars hiring consultants to help your church determine its focus, purpose, mission statement, and all that. But here's some good news for you. God has already given you his mission's statement — and it's the same for every church. It's the Main Thing: "Go and make a disciple."

I suppose you could define a disciple in many different ways, and I know that some have defined the term to justify ministry environments and lifestyles that prop up and propagate our consumerist desires. But I believe that a simple distinction will help us return our focus to the Main Thing: *A consumer is **not** a disciple and a disciple is **not** a consumer!*

Consumerism reflects what Jesus came to call people out of. It's exactly the *opposite* of what Jesus is telling us to go and make! When we get face to face with Jesus,

⇨ he's never going to ask us how many churchgoers we called our own or how good our programs, preaching, or presentations were.
⇨ he's not going to ask for your church budget or care how many friends you had on Facebook.
⇨ he'll not be interested in how many blog hits you had or sermons downloaded.
⇨ he's not going to evaluate how many staff we served with or how many inner-city ministries we supported.
⇨ he won't tell us that we picked the right form of church strategy to try or reference how relevant or culturally savvy our posture was.

The only thing he's going to ask you about your performance (or what he would call your "faithfulness") will be based on a simple measurement:

Did you do all that you could

with what I gave you

to make people like me?

If Jesus brings up any numerical measurements it will probably be more like: "How many people were you able to lead out of their consumerist lifestyle and mentor in the life of the kingdom?" He may even get more specific and ask things like:

⇨ Did you spend the majority of the resources I gave you on things that actually proved to produce change?
⇨ How many people did you lovingly confront out of their stale, pharisaical ways of living, their self-destructive materialism, and their recreational devotion, especially the ones with all the cash?

⇨ Did your buildings contribute to apprenticing people in my ways?

⇨ Are your people considered to be "friends of sinners"? Are they salty? Do they appear as lights in the dark?

⇨ Did your people invest more in heavenly things than earthly things?

⇨ Were they the type of people who drew the curiosity and allure of their friends?

⇨ Did they die to self and worship God with the offer of their lives each day?

⇨ How many people did you challenge and see leave your communities because they had no real interest in following me or serving my purposes?

Please consider these words in 1 Corinthians 3:1 – 15:

Brothers, I could not address you as spiritual but as worldly — mere infants in Christ. I gave you milk, not solid food, for you were not yet ready for it. Indeed, you are still not ready. You are still worldly. For since there is jealousy and quarreling among you, are you not worldly? Are you not acting like mere men? For when one says, "I follow Paul," and another, "I follow Apollos," are you not mere men?

What, after all, is Apollos? And what is Paul? Only servants, through whom you came to believe — as the Lord has assigned to each his task. I planted the seed, Apollos watered it, but God made it grow. So neither he who plants nor he who waters is anything, but only God, who makes things grow. The man who plants and the man who waters have one purpose, and each will be rewarded according to his own labor. For we are God's fellow workers; you are God's field, God's building.

By the grace God has given me, I laid a foundation as an expert builder, and someone else is building on it. But each one should be careful how he builds. For no one can lay any foundation other than the one already laid, which is Jesus Christ. If any man builds on this foundation using gold, silver, costly stones, wood, hay or straw, his work will be shown for what it is, because the Day will bring it to light. It will be revealed with fire, and the fire will test the quality of each man's work. If what he has built survives, he will receive his reward. If it is burned up, he will suffer loss; he himself will be saved, but only as one escaping through the flames.

In the NIV, the heading for this section is "On Divisions in the Church." Paul is addressing one of the root causes of transfer growth — why people find churches, stay for a while, and then leave to find another church. Paul addresses the issue of consumer competition that hinders God's people from becoming disciples. In this Corinthian church people were trying to pick their leaders based on whom they liked the most instead of seeing the bigger picture of what God was trying to produce in them. Thankfully, Paul did not stand for it and called them out. Pastor Paul shows those who play favorites the door. He washes his hands of their immaturity so he doesn't get in trouble with the Head of the church. We would do well to follow his example.

Hebrews 6:1 – 8 has a similar emphasis when it addresses the problem of milk-only, ankle-deep, surface spirituality. In both passages, judgment is mentioned — both for the leader and the learner — if it's not addressed. About the only time the Bible calls us to desire milk is in 1 Peter 2:1 – 3: "Therefore, rid yourselves of all malice and all deceit, hypocrisy, envy, and slander of every kind. Like newborn babies, crave pure spiritual milk, so that by it you may grow up in your salvation, now that you have tasted that the Lord is good." Here Peter allows for milk, but clearly for those who are "craving" God's life. It's for those who are willing to empty themselves of hypocrisy, envy, and deceit. An empty stomach will experience cravings for spiritual truth.

The combined teaching is a staggering call to each of us. We may try to justify our lack of conversion growth by saying, "Well, we all run on the same wheel of providing gathering places for sheep that simply move from one pasture to another." But God's call is clear and can't be watered down or ignored. As leaders in his church, we must get back to the Main Thing and call ourselves and our people to Christ, the one who calls us to stop consuming and start bearing fruit for the kingdom of God.

If developing people *so that they become like Jesus* is our grid for evaluating fruitful ministry, then we have to take an honest look at everything else we've felt pressure to provide and ask ourselves, "Do these activities, services, processes, staff positions, religious ceremonies, and financial resource allocations actually help us reorient someone's life direction so they are growing closer to Jesus?" If they do, that's great! Keep going the direction God is calling you. But if we look at the amount of time, money, and focus that is spent on providing services for people and the results *don't* reflect a fading consumerism in the lives of our people, it's time to take a walk in the woods and talk to the Head of the church. The gravitational pull of consumerism makes it heavier than a crab pot full of wet seaweed!

THE HEART OF THE MATTER IS A MATTER OF THE HEART

Making apprentices out of consumers isn't just a matter of reprogramming. The problem isn't behavioral or methodological — or even ecclesial for that matter. The problem is spiritual. In Galatians 5:16–17 we read, "So I say, live by the Spirit, and you will not gratify the desires of the sinful nature. For the sinful nature desires what is contrary to the Spirit and the Spirit what is contrary to the sinful nature. They are in conflict with each other, so that you do not do what you want."

Despite our cool presentations, powerful personalities, and the biblical mission statements we have plastered all over the sanctuary walls, people have a hard time living for Christ or becoming like Christ because their flesh pulls out a switchblade and tries to fight off God's ways. While God's sanctifying work does give a person a desire for God's ways, it doesn't mean they will easily go toward his ways. I often tell leaders, "Nothing good of the Spirit ever comes naturally or easily." The missional push and the incarnational way of giving your life for others sound really nice, but the reality is that living this way means you don't get what your flesh wants. You don't get to keep all the money. You don't get to do whatever you want with your time. You have to share your house, your stuff, your money, your kids. You have to exchange your ambitions for God's, your kingdom for his, and you must be available for God to interrupt your nicely scheduled day with needs that will cause you to pull your hair out.

The principle is indisputable: the great things of God cost us our life. The more missional you want to be, the more incarnational you're willing to be, the more you release your people out into the world, the more you desire to equip and empower young leaders, the more effective and faithful you want your church to be … the more you'll have to die to your self.

Jesus never intended to start a religion or put a church on every corner. He isn't trying to populate the world or our assemblies with half-baked, halfhearted, religious adherents that reflect half the gospel story. He wants us to take the time to focus on the right things and help develop people to their fullest. Whether your church has eight people or eight thousand, it's time that we begin developing qualitative methods for turning consumers into missionaries, fans into followers, adherents into leaders.

WEANING PEOPLE OFF THE WRONG THINGS

When my first daughter, Alli, was born, I determined that I would give her everything she needed for a full life. I began proving it to her on her second Christmas. Her first Christmas was pretty much a wash, since she just sucked her thumb, wet her pants, and cried. When she reached the age of two, though, I figured she was now ready for Daddy to unload Christmas on her. I went to Toys R Us and bought a vast array of kids' books, toys, cool blankets, little Smurf chairs, blocks, different colored pacifiers, squeaky bath toys, stuffed animals, one of those bouncy dangly thingers where they put their feet through and then jump up and down, and even one of those hanging mobiles with different ornaments for her to play with.

The morning of Christmas, Cheryl and I opened our presents and then I proceeded to open all of Alli's stuff. Each time I'd show her the wrapping and make an excited face, and then I'd hand her the present. In my dad dementia I thought she would grab them excitedly, start tearing the paper off, and then play for an hour with each gift. Yet one after the other, she just looked at me as if to say, "You paid money for this stuff," threw it down on the ground, and stared at me. To say I was put out would be a colossal understatement.

After breakfast, I heard some noise coming from the room where Alli had been napping on the floor. I looked around the table and saw Alli laughing and rolling around in a pile of left over Christmas wrapping paper. As I watched her enthusiasm playing for the next hour, I tried to reshow her the gifts, hoping she'd now be ready to play, but she just wanted the paper. As I added up the amount I spent on all the gifts, it became obvious that I could have saved a few hundred dollars and a lot of frustration if I would have just gotten her a box of wadded up paper.

So can you guess what I got my second daughter, Mckenna, when she turned two? Yep, a wad of paper! Sure enough, she was as happy as her sister. I only wish I had saved Alli's wrapping paper and handed it down. Then I could have saved the extra thirty cents!

So what's my point? *People don't need most of the stuff we give them.* In fact, there seems to be a direct correlation between providing too much and the immaturity that develops when people are given the chance to overindulge. Kevin, one of our pastors, shared last week that one of his sons came to the table for dinner, looked at the plate, and yelled, "Gross!" After sitting down, the food was served, and everyone got a plate full of food except you know who. Kevin laughed as he shared how eventually his boy looked around and said, "Actually, it looks pretty good now."

There's only one way to overcome the problem of consumerism. Not two or three ways, not a program, not a sermon for you to preach or a class for you to teach. Just one way to break the pattern:

You have to remove what they are consuming.

Just as we learned with Alli, if what we give to people isn't appreciated, doesn't inspire them toward the life of Christ, or doesn't lead to any real growth, your only option is to provide less

... or provide something completely different. I realize that for many of us even considering the removal of anything creates some tension, but that's actually my goal. I want to create some tension. All growth requires stretching, struggling, processing, and taking ownership of our responsibilities. That's what maturing is all about.

REMOVE-AND-REPLACE METHOD

Every parent knows that taking anything away from an immature human being immediately produces a negative response. Take a binky or a bottle out of your infant's mouth, give it three seconds, and start running! It's guaranteed that a blood curdling scream, thrashing arms, and uncontrollable kicking are soon to follow. A smart parent learns to insert something better into the infant's mouth at the same time you remove something. Take out the bottle and insert a sugar cookie. Bingo! The same is true when we think about creating disciples out of consumers.

A few months ago, in response to some rapid transfer growth in Adullam (as a result of people finding our book), we decided to take six months and only meet twice a month for larger church gatherings. We did this for two primary reasons. First, we looked at the past and realized that most of our conversion and trans-formation stories happened during spontaneous community time on the weekends. As people bounced off each other, ate together, played together, helped each other, and shared conversation about God, really cool stuff happened. Weekends in Denver are really the best time for this, so we thought it would be missiologically appropriate to give God back the best time of the week for him to work in the ways we had seen him working.

The second reason we made the shift was to help filter through Christians who had "transferred" to us. We noticed that though many people were inspired by the Adullam story and Adullam way of life, they just came to church every week. Consumerism was a deep concern for us and we wanted more for them. So we made this short-term adjustment.

What happened? Well, some people loved it. The ones who had already developed a more scattered way of life told us having two weekends a month to focus solely on engaging the culture around them was awesome. But others struggled with different issues, including many of the concerns mentioned in the following letter:

> Hey Hugh, to get right down to it. Village stuff just doesn't work for us. Any sort of home group — regardless of the name — is just us being at home with kids running around, like any time at home. For us, we need a place to go where we can participate and the kids can be taught and everyone gets a break. We are pretty worn out by the time Sunday rolls around and we enjoy a break from the rest of the week. When Adullam stopped meeting weekly, a few of us families tried to cram into our apartment a few times and it sort of fizzled after that.
>
> Regarding the church gathering, if we didn't have kids I think it would be perfect for us. It's a spontaneous, visceral, and "bare-knuckle" kind of church. I was excited in the beginning about it, and it's still a great group of people. But for our kids we want something more — something long term. The way it works now, I'm not sure Adullam is sustainable for families. I guess for us with three little kids, we need a church where there is weekly consistency and resources for kids. This is good for them and it's good for us. Take care.

Because of my sawed-off military haircut and some candidly tough blogs and writings about church, people assume I'm a heartless drill sergeant who gets his kicks from watching soft evangelicals whimper through the pain of mission. Actually, when I got this email, the Winter-warlock melted. I felt his pain; I admitted to him that I don't like small groups, nor did I enjoy twelve kids running through my house, pooping on my carpet, or screaming while I tried to diatribe through Romans. I didn't blame him at all, and I sincerely wanted to give the guy a hug and start doing church services for him again.

The reality of life does leave people working their backsides off during the week, struggling to find good family time and recovering from all the stress of a busy life. Therefore, on one side of the dilemma, I believe it's an essential ministry for each church to provide a place of spiritual solace for folks. I really mean that.

On the other side of the dilemma of whether or not to expect less and provide a place to just worship and dump the kids off, here's what I heard was happening with two of our "villages" that same week. We do quite a few baby dedications in our normal church services, but one of our "villages" (the name for our incarnational communities) wanted me to come over and facilitate their child's dedication at their home with friends from the neighborhood, their family, and some of their Adullam friends. After the event, I pulled a few of our couples together who all have a boatload of young children and said to them, "So, I heard that some of our families may be struggling with the new Adullam rhythm. I'd love your honest impressions."

For a moment, they all looked at each other with a funny sort of grin, but all at once, they said, "We actually love it!"

"So how do you make it work for the kids and for yourselves?" I asked.

They went on to share how they trade off babysitting with another village so that the adults can take a break together. They have many gatherings where they relationally enjoy each other with the kids all freaking out together, and when they want to have some adult conversation and spiritual time, they either do the child-care switcharoo or they augment their time with men's get-togethers and alternating women's connections.

I eventually let the first guy know what these other communities had done and he loved the idea. My mistake was that I could have helped him avoid the struggle if I had inserted a sugar cookie of new ideas and options before I just pulled the rug out from underneath them.

This week-at-a-glance in the life of Adullam reflects the tension we feel to provide help for the weak who are struggling, while also developing a stronger strain of Christians who live as disciples and nonconsumers. I fear that if we pander to the pressure and lower our expectations, we will miss many opportunities to move our dear friends deeper into the missional mystery. Sometimes I think it's really just a matter of helping people think outside the box and learn from one other. The person who sent the first email may have never considered that he could find solace by trading babysitting time with other couples; and over time, he may even find that integrating kids into mission might be more fun and spiritually formative than just dropping the kids off every Sunday for the next ten years.

These are the artful tensions that every church has to deal with as a result of our consumer-oriented past. Creating a pathway for people to move from fans to followers to fellow kingdom partners is not easy. I don't share this story to suggest that Adullam's more "aggressive" way is the best way for every church. I admit that if I had been more creative in helping people share the stories of how they were making life adjustments to be more missional instead of just expecting them to "toughen up," it's likely that more people would have stayed with us.

As you work through the questions about what you should provide and what you should remove for the sake of growth, remember that you can only be you—the church that God has called you to be. What works in one setting may not work in another.

I suppose that if Adullam had the resources, we would gladly provide a weekly service with multiple times so that anyone struggling to keep their heads above water could have a community to worship with. But Adullam still has no full-time staff or a building of our own. Our pathway of discipleship may not be able to accommodate what a larger, more-resourced church may be able to do, and trying to lower our bar to accommodate hundreds of people would just bury us.

This is why we encourage church planters to be much tougher on the front end of a new church start. When starting a new church, there is usually such a limited amount of time and resources that if the planter spends most of his time rediscipling or renovating existing evangelicals back to mission, he's not going to have much energy left to work with those outside the church. As the church grows, this capacity will grow and the leadership can begin to lower the bar and facilitate different levels of discipleship for various types of people.

Remember that deeper discipleship can't happen from the pulpit or through church programs. It seems to happen best when a leader gives someone personal time. For this reason, pastors and church leaders must assess their ability and their willingness to redistribute their time so they can be available for personal discipleship. For Matt and myself, because of our need to earn the majority of our income outside of Adullam, we only have two days a week available for this. Therefore, we have to restrict our time so we are working either with other leaders or the unchurched. We work with other leaders so that they will be able to make disciples, and we work with the unchurched so that they will get started on the pathway to discipleship. If, however, you are a fully-paid, serving-one-church leader, you will likely have more demands on your time as well as more flexibility and options for investing that time.

We try to live by a simple leadership principle: "Whatever you give your best to will grow." So if you give your best time and resources to the Sunday gathering, you will probably pull off a good one. But if you want to see people move beyond mere attendance, you'll have to shift your time to those things that get them beyond the Sunday service. The deepest level of growth will probably not occur in the Sunday and midweek *gatherings*, but in those activities and tensions related to *scattering*, so try to give your best time to these activities.

In a later chapter we will unpack a process that every church can use that will move people from consumers to contributors, from fans to faithful followers, and from adherents to apprentices.

GUTSY LEADERS

No matter how you break it down, helping develop "nonconsumer Christians" takes guts. Some will read this section with an eye to growing their church. They'll wonder, "Okay, how can I take some of the principles here and tweak them a bit so I don't have to lose people?" If that's you, you aren't facing the music. Yes, people do want to grow and become more like Jesus, but there are also many who don't. Some will love it when you pull the bottle of milk out of their mouth and will hunger for a greater challenge, but others will begin gasping for air as soon as the sweet milk is removed, groping for another bottle, and they will leave your church before they've had a chance to taste a better way. You *will* lose people.

Jesus often had "crowds of fans following him," and then the very next day he was back down to a few disciples. Always remember the Main Thing! God knows that fifty committed apprentices will out-serve, out-love, out-sacrifice, and out-faithful two thousand fans, but along the way you will take hits and you will start to wonder if things wouldn't be easier if you could just provide church services for people.

Adullam now has three hundred apprentices, but that's not the entire story. We've had another five hundred people come through our process who decided there was an easier way and left. Do I lament the loss of those people? Of course! But I have a feeling that I'd be feeling a different kind of pain if we had tried to keep everyone from leaving.

CHOOSE YOUR PAIN

If you choose the nonconsumer path, you will face tension. Now there's a life changing statement. "No kidding, Halter, tell me something new." Every leader we've ever coached speaks about tension as if it's air. It's just what you breathe as a leader.

But there are two types of tension we can breathe. One type of tension, the kind most have been fighting is, "How do I keep people coming to my church?" You'll never win with this kind of tension. You'll never feel done, there will never be enough people, and you'll never stop worrying about losing their nominal commitment. This kind of tension leaves you relieved for a few minutes after your Sunday service because numbers were up, but by 3:00 p.m. Monday you are doing mental and emotional jumping jacks wondering how to avoid losing your momentum.

The other tension you can deal with is more helpful. It's the tension that comes from asking, "How do I help every person become more like Jesus?" Like the first tension, this one will also never go away, but you will see some payoff that you won't get with tension #1. The payoff is that you'll begin to see people struggling with the issues that matter. You'll hear stories of changing decisions, of habits being adjusted, and of faith being stretched. On the high end, you will watch people taking responsibility, not only for their own growth but also for the growth of others. Where once they relied on you to relieve their burdens and prop them up, they will begin carrying the weight of others. Some of the best will eventually leave because they are responding to the call of God on their own lives.

One way or another you have to decide what kind of tension you want to work with. If you don't lead well, you will struggle with the wrong kind of tension as you try to keep things from falling apart; but if you lead the right way, you will need to get into the mess of real struggles and probably lose your best leaders to other missions. Tension is inevitable—but you can choose which kind of tension you want to live with as a leader.

This is one of those decisions that we really hope you take seriously and one that we should all be able to agree on: the gospel is costly! Leaders face the pressure of pride and peer respect, the pressure of financial survival, the pressure of living up to the expectations of those who hold positions of power over us, and our own self-created pressures, where at the end of each day, as we turn off the light and lie in bed, we silently wonder if Jesus is really pleased with us. Add to all of this the real and constant attack of satanic forces, and it should be clear that we need to stop fighting over how to do church and just be thankful we're in the honorable position of leading people who belong to God.

No one can escape the pains and pressures of leading others. But I believe this reality should drive us to create a new kind of peer pressure, a pressure to live and work for the things that not only make us proud to follow Jesus, giving us peace and joy as we lead, but that actually throw back the plans of the underworld and bring a smile to God's face.

Pastoring is as much about protecting the flock as it is about growing a flock. It's about pushing them and challenging them instead of pandering to them. Ultimately, it's time for leaders to be consumed in a struggle against consumerism. Our collective calling as leaders is to create spiritual pathways for people so they can come out of their old life and find the new life of Christ. To this end, the next chapter may help.

CHAPTER 4

Spiritual Formation for Missional Churches

THIS MAY SURPRISE YOU, but I've never felt like a very spiritual man. Although I have always had strong beliefs and remained faithful to the common Christian life, my walk with God has been more based on obedience than what many would call deep spiritual formation. My obedience-based, just-get-it-done, don't-expect-much Christianity was confirmed and entrenched in my seminary experience. I got kicked out of three classes within two years. During one theology class I challenged the instructor's hypothesis that wine in the New Testament was really grape juice; I was asked to leave. Two weeks later, in a Greek class, the instructor asked me to remove my brand-new Tiger running shoes because he said the fluorescent colors were distracting the other students from his presentation. I asserted that maybe it was because his teaching style was not as colorful, and that also got me sent out.

I eventually moved across town to another seminary to find a more palatable academic situation, but my woes continued. I enrolled in a "contemplative spirituality class." No, I didn't choose it; it was required. Each class taught us different ways of listening to God. Sometimes we just sat in class and were led in quiet listening prayer, but most of the time they sent us off to walk around the campus to try to hear from God on our own. The last twenty minutes were set aside to meet together and share how God had spoken to us. Each week I dreaded the "sharing time" because I really struggled to hear anything. "Sorry, Dr., all I got was a good walk ... again." Eventually, the gentle professor invited me into his office and suggested that maybe it would be better for the class and my own progress if I joined the military, maybe as a Navy Seal, or a sniper, or something more engaging.

I figured I'd probably get kicked out of the military too, so instead I chose to go on staff with Youth For Christ, eventually planted our first church, and have ever since wondered why God, in his strange cosmic humor, called such an "unspiritual man" to be a pastor. My wife has felt the same. With encouragement from some mentors, she decided to attend a spiritual formation week at a monastic retreat center. She wasn't too excited about it, but I told her that some people she really liked would be there and that they'd have a lot of fun. She went ... reluctantly. Two days later I got a phone call from her. She was whispering and said, "Get me out of here! They don't let you talk here, at all ... not even during meals. We have to just sit there and stare at each other. I can't take it and I'm hiding behind this big Jesus statue in the front quad, so come pick me up, NOW!" I knew that Cheryl's primary gifting was "talking," but I still tried to encourage her to go the distance and push through the weekend. She made it, but I definitely got an earful when she got home.

I'm bringing this up because I believe that finding the beauty and power of the missional/incarnational church isn't just about new ways of leading the church. I think the dilemma of the church is really a dilemma of the people. To put it simply, I think it's an issue of spiritual formation. In some ways, I believe that even the gravity toward consumerism is simply a symptom of how bored our people are with the basic Christian experience. I've heard it a thousand times if I've heard it once: "Isn't there more than just Bible study, personal devotions, and helping the poor?" Why don't we see more similarities between the stories we read about in Scripture and what our lives feel like here and now? Why does it feel as if there's a Grand Canyon-sized chasm between my spiritual life and my real life?

This last week I was training forty pastors in Boulder, Colorado. I started a session on spiritual formation with this question: "What is your greatest frustration in ministry?" They broke up into small groups and then I solicited their answers. They were exactly the same answers I've heard in every setting in every country from pastors of every conceivable form and focus of church. Here were some of their frustrations:

⇨ Trying to make a materialistic, distracted, dysfunctional person into a disciple.

⇨ I can't seem to get our people to actually believe in their beliefs.

⇨ My people are mostly Pharisees, and I think I may be one too.

⇨ Our church is nothing but a consumer trap. I consume them and they consume me. I've come to expect nothing more than entry-level attendance and adherents to doctrinal beliefs, and in turn they expect me not to rock the boat.

⇨ People don't believe what Jesus believed and they don't act like he acted.

⇨ I can't seem to get our small groups to get beyond Bible studies.

⇨ I don't even want my non-Christians to meet most of my parishioners.

⇨ I'm so dry spiritually, I'm not even sure how to lead my people anywhere, and our worship service is about as inspirational as the chapel service on the *Titanic*.

⇨ Our people just don't expect to see God do much any-more, and I'm not sure I do either.

Then I put together a list of everything you hear when you ask laypeople to express their frustrations with spiritual formation practices. Here's what you will often hear:

⇨ It's guilt-driven or duty-driven.
⇨ It's always about church attendance, Bible study, worship, and prayer.
⇨ It's rarely integrated with normal life.
⇨ It suggests that I do a lot of things alone, by myself or in quiet places.
⇨ It's cognitive and study-focused and rarely captivates my emotions and desires.
⇨ It makes sin management the main goal instead of becoming more like Jesus.
⇨ It tends to focus on "not doing things" instead of helping us focus on "the things Jesus wants us to do."
⇨ At the end of every attempt to "grow spiritually," I feel more self-judgment because I fail and I tend to become more judgmental with others who also fail.
⇨ And here's the one that most people bring up: *Spiritual formation practices always seem to extract us from the real world as opposed to helping us integrate with the world.*

THE NEW OPPORTUNITY OF SPIRITUAL FORMATION

So where's the "good news" in all of this? People will naturally gravitate toward experiences that are meaningful, and the most meaningful experience a person can have in this life is to feel connected with God—to know that God is leading their lives, challenging them, interacting with them, and using them to change the world. The common message of controlling sin, going to church, reading your Bible, journaling, and praying is that it just does not paint a compelling enough picture to keep people engaged spiritually, nor does it actually produce an active spirituality where people see God and grow.

There is an open opportunity that every church has at this unique time of transition. If we can start to redefine spiritual formation as *becoming* like Jesus instead of just *knowing* about Jesus, and if we can provide a pathway for their spiritual development *along the way* of real life instead of just giving a weekly call to "do better," I think we'll find a new stride for our own leadership and our people.

We will try to give a framework for this shortly, but let's start by reminding ourselves what spiritual formation is and what the goals are in spiritual formation.

No matter how people try to communicate or define spiritual formation, most would agree that the final goal is that people become like Jesus. Of course, what it means to be like Jesus gives us some wiggle room, but this angle may help us get some clarity on the definition of a disciple. A disciple is *not* someone who stays the same. A disciple is someone struggling to live a life of heartfelt love and obedience to the Father, living and dying for the higher purposes of God's kingdom. Disciples are called out of their selfish ambitions, and they understand that the longer they follow Jesus, the more uncomfortable they will be and the more sacrifice and effort it will require.

Disciples expect tension! They wake up each day expecting that the Father will lead and guide their day; they have given ownership of all they have back to God, for him to direct. They trust God for supernatural provision; they let faith in God win out over safety, common sense, or worldly wisdom; moreover, their relationship with God is deeply integrated with a community of other believers, and they have many relationships with people in the non-Christian culture. They view Scripture as God's message to a missional people instead of a series of self-help slogans; they pray out of desperation for the circumstances they find themselves in as they walk in the world instead of simply doing things in isolation; and they view the church as a community of fellow passionaries joyfully gathering to see each other, as opposed to strangers they sing songs with once a week.

Maybe this reworking of God's basic instruction to us may help us reenvision what spiritual formation is:

To those who are trying to figure out the life of God, both to them who love and worship me [Jesus], and even to those who struggle with doubt, God has given me global authority out of heaven to change earth. So stop living your small life and jump into the challenge of going everywhere to call people out of their self-indulged, self-focused, meaningless consumer-existence. Throw them under the waters of regenerated life and teach and model, enjoy, and offer to others the beautiful but revolutionary life of the kingdom. Settle for nothing less! And you better believe I'm in every breath you breathe and every step you take, and I'll be the first person you see as soon as my full, pure kingdom comes crashing into this dark kingdom for the last and final time. (Matt. 28:16–20, Hugh's expanded paraphrase)

I feel uncomfortable paraphrasing Scripture, but I fear that we can so quickly lose the true meaning of Jesus' words through our familiarity with them as we read them over and over. Just saying that a disciple is a "nonconsumer" doesn't really grab me by the throat. But actually communicating that every believer can become like Jesus, not only in theological understanding but in personality, gifting, actions, and influence should turn people around in their tracks!

Regardless of our specific church form, the process of spiritual formation in our church must help move people out of consumerism and toward the life, actions, and devotion of Jesus. This process *must* call for change, challenge the status quo, and guide people through the tension of being counter-culture kingdom people. By studying how Jesus formed his friends, spiritual formation can become more than an isolated, extractional drudgery that someone is forced to add to an already overburdened life. Being formed into Christ's image is an invitation to follow him — to *really* follow him.

The allure of Jesus-like life is what every soul craves, and the churches that expand their definition of spiritual formation and invite people into active processes will win the day. If anything legitimizes a pastor's paycheck, it's that we truly shepherd the sheep—not into little safe cloisters where the best part of the day is when the shepherd dumps a bunch of mush on the ground to consume, but truly leading the sheep out into the sunlight of opportunity and world transformation. It's what Paul would have called, "equipping the saints to do the work of the ministry." This equipping must move people from the classroom and the sanctuary back into homes, the streets, and the natural places of connection with the world.

In *The Tangible Kingdom*, we shared a simple diagram to help people integrate their lives in this manner in the context of community. This is essentially how we communicate and develop a basic kingdom DNA. Many people assume that our primary purpose in coaching our folks to this end is *evangelism*. Although we do believe that whenever you find people integrating community, communion, and mission, the kingdom becomes tangible and people find Christ, our primary purpose is really spiritual formation, discipleship, or apprenticeship after Christ. We ask people to live this way for themselves!

As a quick overview, the *community* sphere represents a more biblical and inclusive sense of social arrangements where very "unlike"

people can all feel a deep sense of belonging. We'd say it's a place where saints (Christians) and sojourners (spiritually disoriented God-seekers) can actually be together. The *mission* sphere represents the more holistic gospel issues of caring for the poor and the marginalized, and essentially doing acts in the world and with people who represent God's heart in heaven. And the *communion* sphere represents those activities that relate to our connection or communion with God. I bring this up again, because it may help us understand why our forms of spiritual formation don't really yield much fruit and why I struggled for so long to figure out how to grow with God.

THREE MOST COMMON SPIRITUAL FORMATION BLUNDERS

There are three primary blunders in the area of spiritual formation that most of us have experienced, maintained, or promoted in our ministries.

The first is simply not having any formation process at all. This may seem surprising, but it's alarming how many churches act as though people will just become like Jesus through osmosis or through a sermon they have heard. We must recognize that Jesus himself walked for years with a small band of followers, and they still looked like the B-team when he left this earth. We'll talk about the process that Jesus used in a minute, but if anything changes the way you do church after reading this story, I hope it's that you'll stop assuming that people will just grow without an actual process. They won't.

Formation of the spirit is a dogfight, and it requires both an air war and a ground war. The *air war* is what the leadership say, speak, challenge, exhort, put on their website, and teach their people — whether from behind the pulpit or sitting around tables at Starbucks. The *ground war* is the actual trenches that are built as causeways for active learning and communal reflection. The key to winning the fight is that both offensives work together in tandem to fight against the gravity of the consumer-oriented, fan-friendly, short-sheeted spiritual formation most churches constantly succumb to.

The second blunder is to have a lopsided process. In college I worked at a juvenile penitentiary during the summers. We were trained in a variety of social work, psychology, and family dynamics, but we also had to learn basic life-saving techniques, even canoe safety. During the training they made three people go out into a canoe and learn to keep it balanced. One drill required that the triad of would-be sailors take turns changing positions in the canoe. It required that the team learn to communicate, stay balanced, and work together. I'd say that our team did great at every part, except we just couldn't overcome one unique dilemma of our crew. One guy was about 350 pounds! No matter what we tried to do to offset his overage, whenever he made even the slightest move, we'd all go flying overboard. Our intentions were great, our desires were in line, and we didn't want to keep going overboard, but the weight of one person kept us capsizing. This illustrates the most common issue.

In classic spiritual formation circles, most practices are inside the Communion circle (Scripture, prayer, meditation, worship, church attendance, Sabbath experiences, etc.). The only addition to our normal process of formation might come from what we call the Community circle, where we've asked people to be in small groups or accountability groups with other believers. Most transfer growth is focused on this sphere as well. People, good-hearted or selfish, are subconsciously asking, "Can your church help me grow with God?" They base their search for a church on who they think can best teach them Scripture, best help them worship, and best teach their children. Again, all of this goes on with the assumption that spiritual formation primarily takes place inside a cognitive learning environment (the God-zone).

The problems first arise in what many now call assimilation ministries. Awhile back, assimilators touted that people make a decision about whether or not they'll come back to a church within the first ninety seconds of their visit. So we work hard to make sure that our greeters are friendly and our music is appropriate, and the coffee is nice and hot so that we won't lose people right away. Granted, there may be some sociological factors behind all this, and most assuredly Jesus wouldn't have said, "Go out of your way to make people feel awkward and uncomfortable." But we need to realize that this line of thinking is really about the church *service* and whether or not people may come back to our *service* again. It does not, however, determine whether or not someone actually wants to follow Christ. It only addresses whether they want to get up the next week, put on nice clothes, and drive back to our church. If that's not our primary goal, then perhaps focusing too much on assimilation is the wrong approach.

Again, we must remember that the main goal of spiritual leadership is not about trying to keep people in our churches or win their loyalty over another church around the corner. We have to keep pushing back toward the real process of making people into little Jesuses. Assimilation is *not* the same as spiritual formation.

In fact, by way of warning, if we focus primarily on the Communion circle and Christians start hanging out primarily with other Christians, what naturally forms is not a kingdom-oriented Jesus people, but modern-day Pharisees. You'll get people with lots of head knowledge, lots of experience spending time in religious environments, myopic social/spiritual/relational circles, and a strong focus on obedience and outward behavior. A lack of contact with the lives of worldly, non-Christian peasants will almost always produce a fervently religious person. You may end up with the opposite of what Jesus actually wants to produce in our churches.

This leads us to the third blunder: minimizing the barriers between the spheres, acting as if they are not really there, and failing to provide intentional ways to help people overcome them. People who come to our churches looking for a place to *commune* would probably love to live a life of *mission*, giving sacrificially and generously to people in need and giving time to the poor and oppressed, but they've dug themselves into a hole through materialism. Others would love to be a part of an *inclusive community,* but they just can't seem to die to their individualism. Such barriers represent the fight of the Spirit to win out over the flesh and the battle against a globally satanic, organized, and intentional world system that traps our people, making them one-sided, no-sided, and dead spiritually.

If the spiritual formation process in your church is weighted toward the Communion circle, you'll tend to produce Pharisees. If you put too much weight in the Mission circle, you'll tend to create social workers. And if you overemphasize inclusive Community, you'll have some great parties but no one will move toward Christ or toward maturity in the Christian faith.

The key to healthy spiritual formation is to balance, empower, and invest equally between the three spheres, creating transitions that help people leap over or bust through the barriers, and self-evaluating with the goal of creating experiential kingdom apprentices instead of cognitive disciples or flimsy-faith fans.

The process Jesus gives to us certainly includes the Communion sphere (Jesus modeled all of these practices), but we must also learn to give the other two circles equal weight. If they aren't balanced, the spiritual formation of our people will be stunted and they will live a malnourished spiritual life. They must learn how to live out their faith in relationship with pagans, and learn that pure religion that pleases God involves service to people. I don't want to minimize the importance of Communion; I know that many people really do hear from God in silence and meditation, and I'm surely not suggesting that we replace the idea of quiet times with "loud times"; but I think it's time for us to swing the pendulum a bit to the other two circles.

SPIRITUAL FORMATION FRAMEWORK

In a moment, we'd like to suggest a four-part process that any form of church can use for spiritual formation. We believe it takes a much more holistic approach to forming people into Jesus people. But first, we want to suggest that Jesus' process was much simpler than you may think. Imagine you have a moment with Jesus over a latte and you ask, "So … it seemed pretty hard to help Western Christians become like you. In fact, it seemed like the more we walked the talk or pushed them beyond the pews, they took off. So how did you develop people to be so darn committed to your cause?"

In my feeble mind, I can't get past Jesus saying something like, "To get people to be like me is actually the toughest thing in the whole world to do. It was the same for me back in my day. So all I did was invite people to follow me, go where I went, watch me do what I did, experience what I experienced, and then send them off to do the same. After that, I usually debriefed or helped them work through the difficulty and the tensions, and I taught them about the kingdom, the Father, and my way of life. When it didn't go too well, I confronted them; when they got bummed out, I encouraged them. I always raised the bar much higher for them than they would have raised it for themselves; I forced them to learn together in community. In fact, I left them because I knew that if I allowed them to always feel safer by me, they'd never learn to trust the Holy Spirit, to work together, or to take ownership of my mission."

Now I admit — this is just Hugh's lame daydream, but you'll notice that it includes many aspects of the process Jesus used to develop people — watching, visual learning, questioning, struggling, confronting, calling people out, raising the bar, assimilating people, and using trial and error, community, challenge, ownership, and a death and growth cycle. Each of these aspects must reemerge in the spiritual formation process of any missional church.

CREATING A NONCONSUMER PROCESS OF APPRENTICESHIP

As we've looked at mega-churches and micro-churches that have this more holistic discipleship process, we've noticed that each one has a deliberate process that keeps them on track and minimizes consumer tendencies. Another way of looking at it is to say that they've created more of an apprenticeship environment. This concept may be helpful because any apprenticeship process is usually highly interactive, based on real life, and has more of a mentorship aspect where people are guided into proficiency in the area they wish to learn.

What we'd like to do now is present a framework that may help spur your creativity as you form your own spiritual apprenticeship process. Our way is not *the* way, but it may get you started. Keep in mind that this process is primarily for *reorienting* Christians back into the Mission circle. Since most church growth in America is transfer growth, the greatest need is to reorient people. The average sojourner who comes to faith will probably have intuitively moved through this framework as part of their conversion experience. We'll explain more about that at the end of this chapter.

Observance

Any volunteer-led movement—whether it's the military, a local initiative, a school board, a missions project, a monastic community, or a church—works best when people are given time to be inspired by what they see and then have the opportunity to participate when asked to be involved. The length of commitment and the depth of ownership people have depend on whether or not they knew exactly what joining up would be like, and whether or not they were given pathways to move at their own pace to grow more deeply into whatever it is they were emotionally pulled toward.

This is what *observance* is all about.

It's a season of time where people decide if *their* story matches *your* story. A good way to view it is as a dating process, where they, as well as you, get to see if you are mutually attracted to similar values, convictions, rhythms of life, worship, and mission. And of course, it's a time where you get to see if your attraction grows toward each other.

In our second year as a church, we were meeting at a local park for a baptism gathering. The place was packed with our folks and your typical boaters, jet skiers, and sunbathers. We had a meaningful time in the water and a great all-day barbeque with sand volleyball and kids' games, and many folks brought friends to join us. One couple was from the seminary. A local mentor suggested they try Adullam and let me know they'd be coming. I greeted them as they came in the morning and then later went back to talk to them while their kids were wading in the lake. We did the normal small talk, and then I said, "So, Wes mentioned that you guys may be coming by and that you're looking for a church of some kind. Is there anything I can tell you or any questions I can answer for you?"

I thought the cool baptism and untraditional posture of our folks would have already won them over, but Mark said, "Actually, we're really not sure about church or what we're looking for, if anything. If we have any questions we'll be sure to call you later." The look on his face and the tone of his voice essentially told me, "Back off, dude." So I backed off, assuming that would be the last time I saw them. It's now been two years since that fateful meeting, and last week Mark joined our staff and preached his first sermon in Adullam.

At the same time, however, I can remember hundreds of people who have come in, apparently loved us, resonated with our methodology and style, and, according to their words, "found a home," only to be gone within four to twelve weeks with no word or returned emails.

All these scenarios expose why pastors often pull their hair out trying to figure out where the balance is in "selling the vision of the church" and assimilating and attracting people to our churches versus simply trusting God to build our communities. Looking back over twenty years of pastoral ministry, I can add up thousands of hours spent trying to get people to come with us or be a part of us, only to have them leave us later, some after another hundred hours invested in trying to work out some values or vision differences. Working with church planters is even more telling. In most cases, the planter assumes that they have a small army of servants ready to take on the underworld, only to find most of them gone after two years.

If there's anything that has been overlooked regarding the establishment of the early faith communities, it's that people were able to watch the communities from a distance and choose for themselves if it was for them. The experiences of the early Christians were inspiring but scary, and you don't get the impression that the first set of pastors spent much of their time preparing a greeter team or an assimilation team for the massive onslaught of church shoppers. Everyone in the city knew by either watching or listening exactly what the Christian communities were all about, and by the time someone showed interest in joining, they had observed them for a while and were ready to be part of the community of faith. Giving people the freedom to watch and observe is something of a lost concept, but it needs to be reborn in our churches.

Jesus on Observance

If you acknowledge Jesus' wisdom, intentionality, vision for the world and the church, his absolute perception into the human psyche and emotions, and his pure motivation for people, it may help us understand how we can make *his* ways of spiritual formation *our* ways, especially when it comes to the idea of *observance*. In John 3, a Pharisee named Nicodemus comes to Jesus and says, "Rabbi, we know that you are a teacher come from God, for no one can do these signs that you do unless God is with him." This man, who kept his head down and spent time learning his doctrine, theology, Jewish history, and the traditions, is now looking up; he has clearly been watching Jesus! Throughout the four gospels, various Pharisees come to Jesus after they observe him breaking Jewish religious laws and healing people, or after they overhear his teachings. They are also checking him out.

On another instance, Jesus has a crowd following him, "gawking" at him, and he turns around and begins challenging them on the hard issues of discipleship (see Luke 9:57–62). In the midst of yet another crowd of fans, Jesus notices a guy named Zacchaeus up above the crowd in a tree watching him, and he challenges him to join him (Luke 19:1–10). Finally, in Acts 5:13 we read that people held the first communities in "high regard," but "no one dared to join them." In each of these examples, people are *observing* what Jesus and his followers are like and watching what they do together.

Somehow, Jesus had a way of cutting through the throngs of people to pick out the ones who seemed a bit more curious than the rest. Jesus wasn't all that interested in keeping or growing the crowd. He didn't waste time and emotional energy planning programs or leading strategic efforts trying to draw people to a consumer-oriented environment. And he wasn't too worried about opening the front door or closing the back door of his group of disciples. Instead, Jesus preferred to allow people to observe him and make that extra effort to figure him out. He knew that the real seekers would keep pursuing him and wouldn't be satisfied until they had come to him.

Like the example of Zacchaeus, when Jesus did notice someone who really wanted to see him or learn from him, he moved toward that person. I think this is an approach we can model, having appropriate observance pathways. An observance period allows people a chance to develop genuine interest, which in turn gives the community the time to hear their story and find the most meaningful ways of initiating them into congregational structures and the rhythms and mission of the church.

"What about all the others who didn't stay with you?" you may be asking. Well, as I said, because we hadn't articulated a clear pathway for people or given them time to observe what we were like, I do think we lost a few people whom we could have kept, but I have also learned that few really want what we want. Sadly, many people really are satisfied living as consumers, and they are just looking for a place to hold their beliefs together and to provide a sense of belonging relationally. In other words, all they want are some sermons and some friends. Now, neither of these is bad in and of itself, and any person who grows into a community ought to find that these come naturally; but if they are the only two reasons people are coming to our church, we have to realize they aren't looking for transformation, either for themselves or for the world.

The only way to really help the curious move forward is to allow them some time to observe, struggle, and work through personal issues that may have hung them up at their last church. Remember, if people have come to your church from another experience or have taken a several-year timeout, they will have some stories! Invariably, something caused them to leave, check out, tap out, or Sabbath on turbo.

Hearing Your Story

Here are a few key aspects of any observance experience. First, there must be a time for them to hear your story and the story of the church. Before we wrote *The Tangible Kingdom*, we did coffee after coffee with folks and told them our story. Now that the book is out, we just tell them to read about it. Every story, if told honestly, reveals values, dreams, plans, and prejudices and gives people a more realistic idea of what life would be like if they were to jump into our mission. Hearing your story is critical because it moves a nebulous, general church expectation to a narrative that they can find themselves in. When I tell people about our life, our struggle with church, our family dilemma dealing with severe disabilities with our son, our work outside of church to provide for our family, and then all of our vision for what a church could be, I know they are not only getting a vision; they are deciding if they want to be with me personally.

Jesus held his cards pretty tight for a while, but as his plan began to unfold, he let people know and discover his story. Early on he healed or talked to someone and then encouraged them not to tell anyone; later he let them in on the reality of his story. If they didn't ask who he was, he'd prompt it: "Who do you say I am?" Then later, he let them know what life with him would be like: "You'll have no place to lay your head; you're going to have to prioritize me over your traditions and family; you're going to have to bear a cross of your own if you go with me. You'll have to become last and serve people all the time, because I will be following whatever I see my Father doing; and he's working hard all the time, so you can expect that too." Jesus wanted them to know his story.

In observance, I want people to hear the stories of as many of our people as possible because people are not drawn to mission statements anymore. They are drawn to stories like their own. Leery, tapped-out Christians need to hear from people who know what it's like to be tapped out. Jaded leaders need to hear from other jaded leaders, and confused people, broken people, and curious people need to find others like them. For *observance* to work, you as the leader need to change your posture. Stop acting as if you are a desperate leader trying to get people to come to your church. Stop worrying about assimilating them. Be yourself, tell your story, and passionately say what your heart feels; and if people are sniffing the same air, you will find some fellow kingdom sojourners. If you attract anyone without giving them the real spiel, you'll get what you deserve and find yourself doing a lot of exit interviews later.

Hearing Their Story

Second, we use this season of observance to hear *their* story. As mentioned above, every person is a unique context of values, dreams, plans, hang-ups, hurts, and expectations. Every person has some incredible gifts that must be used and resources that must be shared, but also great brokenness and pain that, if not understood, will eventually hurt others and paralyze missional community. Richard Rohr once said, "If the pain of your story is not transformed, it will be transmitted."

Observance isn't just a way of weeding out the church shoppers or sending the ones you don't like to mess with to another church. It's really about knowing your people. It's how you can discern the best way to move them forward spiritually and how much time needs to be given to reforming, reigniting, counseling, or training. You won't know how to move them until you know them.

Spiritual formation modeled after the life of Christ is one huge story, and it should absolutely inspire people out of their mundane worldview, but it should also scare the south side of Hades out of them. If you're worried about how to keep halfhearted, recreational Christians from leaving your church, I fear you've lost the big story. People should feel lucky to get to be a part of your mission and your church, and you'll be equally fortunate that they someday acknowledge they would rather serve with you and your people over any other church in the city. Give them time to decide and give yourself some time to let God work in them. It will not only save you hundreds of wasted hours over the course of a year, but you'll end up with the people with whom God has decided to build his church.

Observance

Dating

"Call Out"

Preparation

Mentoring

Prayer of Blessing
(Public Sending)

Participation

Coaching

Commissioning
(Membership)

Partnership

Empowerment

Transitions: The Key to Spiritual Growth

Although it may be helpful to see the four phases of reorienting Christians back into mission and apprenticeship, the most important aspects are actually transition points. Just as a jeep can get high centered or someone can get stuck in a rut, intentional transitions help get folks "unstuck." Creative, sensitive, and timely transitions will help you overcome this dilemma.

First transition point: Call them out. In Adullam, our first transition is simply a "callout." We invite anyone who has observed us for awhile to join us for a "Welcome to Adullam" evening with other observers. We put on a nice meal, light some candles, decant some nice wine, and have a lovely talk about the Adullam vision, recap our story, give them time to express how they have processed their spiritual journey in light of ours — and then we lay the hammer on them! At end of the evening I'll say something like this:

> First, we want you all to know that we're honored you have resonated with what you've seen so far, and we think it's really cool you've made it through a tough time of observance. We didn't want to move too fast toward you, and we didn't feel it was the right thing to ask you to do anything. We just wanted to give you time to see if God may be calling you to us. The best way to think of Adullam is as a mission to Denver. We are all done with "going to church" and we are really serious about trying to become a church to this city. Mission is what God's called us to and church is something he builds us into as we go with him into the world. So if at this point you are ready to come and die with us, we'd love to have you with us.

You should see their faces when I use the word "die." I think most expect me to invite them into a membership process or plug them into a small group. Apparently, most who grew up in a church have never been asked to give their lives for Jesus. What may have been missed as I share this point of our process is that I'm not calling people to give their lives for something I haven't. I'm not asking them to give a few hours of volunteer time to help us build our church. Although the message is hard to hear, it comes across like a friend calling another friend to a higher purpose.

I have learned that people love to get called out as long as they are being called in the context of friendship and from those who have already made the commitment. Most of the ruts people fall into occur because we haven't called them to anything greater. A great quote I once learned describes this process perfectly: "In the absence of vision, pettiness prevails." In other words, when someone is bored, he or she will start critiquing, judging, making problems, and consuming. Sometimes, all it takes to change things around is to take someone out to coffee and acknowledge the legitimate gifts you see in them, and then give them a few good ideas of where they can begin to use their gifts. "Come and die" may not work with everyone, but believe me, it is very effective when you have the right people!

"Yah, I get that," you may say, "but who has time to call everyone out?" Well, that's the hard shift leaders have to make in their own lives. Imagine you took the thirty to forty hours a week the average pastor spends on preparing the worship service for the consumers. Consider how many people you could have a profound prophetic conversation with if you used even half of those hours helping them move beyond the weekly church service. Try to remember how life-reorienting it was when a coach or an employer pulled you into his office, called you to a higher level of responsibility, and told you what they saw in you. It's no different in a church setting.

Every year I invite about twenty people into a leadership-mentor group. I choose people who I know have huge capacity, but for whatever reason they seem stuck in nowhere land. I meet with them once a month for eight months, and every time they come alive and begin to take their calling and lives more seriously. When I prepare my speaking and teaching for these gatherings, I make sure that I am consistently calling them out, and we now use these regular gatherings of mentor groups to call everyone to live for something bigger and to die to themselves.

Calling people to leave their nets, to prioritize God's mission over their own, to live by faith, to take up their cross, to deny self, and to seek first God's kingdom and righteous life is what seekers are so desperate to hear. Let me challenge you to take a risk and start inviting people as Jesus did. Begin personally to invite higher-level leaders to your home, give them your best time, and trust that if you're honest about how hard Christianity is and how their lives will change, God will build his church — the one he's entrusted to you to lead well.

If you're wondering where we lose people, it's almost always during the time of observance or right after this first transition point, where they are called to commit to the real deal. I think it makes perfect sense that Christians who don't really want to follow Christ would balk here. Even though it's always hard to see people drift off, I believe it's a sign of faithful leadership and congregational health to be honest with people up front. Raise the bar early in the reorienting process and you'll feel much less pressure as you go forward.

Preparation

Since I began this chapter by giving you a few seminary stories, I thought I'd add one more. During a New Testament survey class, I remember a poignant dialogue between the students over the topic "Why did Jesus do so many miracles?" A Miller-Lite beer commercial scenario began because half the class thought Jesus did them because he was fulfilling Scripture, and the other half thought it was because he wanted to make the religious elite angry. Realizing that both sides had some good points and knowing I tend to enjoy a good fight, I raised my hand and said, "You know, there may be one other reason Jesus did so many miracles. Maybe he did them because he knew that by helping people, he would win their hearts." It was silent for a few awkward seconds and then the earlier dualistic argument started right back up as if "dumb-guy Halter" wasn't even close to the hermeneutically correct answer.

Over the years, I've come back to my answer and actually believe that it is one of the main reasons Jesus helped so many people with real life answers. He knew that unless he won the hearts of the peasants, they would never consider changing their life trajectory or religious biases, or move past their personal fears. I think the same situations exist today. In this spiritual formation process, we're setting a framework that takes the heart seriously. We all remember what our parents, coaches, or teachers have said to those that were slacking off: "Your heart's not in it!" Or maybe you remember the slogan of the high school football team portrayed in the television show *Friday Night Lights*. In what has become a well-known slogan contextualized for an underdog band of adolescent gridiron fanatics, just before taking on a better team, the coach inspires them with this soliloquy: "Clear eyes ... full heart ... can't lose."

The reason we suggest another season of *preparation* before you just dive in with people is for this one simple issue—people have lost their heart for church and church-related stuff. It's not that they've lost their heart for God, for loving Jesus—it's just the religious stuff. They've grown weary of more books to read, another program to try, another attempt at "outreach," or another impassioned sermon to give money for anything. They're tired of volunteering in the nursery or going through an eight-week training manual on "how to be a greeter." The last one is probably an overstatement, but if you've really been talking to people, you'll realize that millions of Christians are hanging on by a thread of loyalty; but their fingers are beginning to slip, their eyes are dull, and their hearts long to see some real change, have some real impact, and experience some personal transformation in their own lives again.

Preparation is a short-term experience that communicates, "Look, we're not here to get you to help us build our kingdom; we're here as a church leadership to help you find your heart again." Preparation is a commitment to mentor them through heart issues as well as beginning the reorientation back to missional living. When people are processing Adullam, I always let them know that Adullam will be hard, it won't carve out for them an easy path, it won't provide all the services they may have gotten from the next church; but we will provide a pathway for them to find God in fresh ways out in the streets, in their family, and in the lives of those they really care about.

Jesus did his miracles on the streets in plain view. The word spread and more people showed up because they hoped for some transformation. He delivered. Religious people started to take a fresh look at their traditions, their family heritage, and their existing social network, and they subconsciously compared it to this new world Jesus was speaking of and modeling for them. The less religious or non-Jewish folks who began to come to faith also had to rethink everything.

Sure, many of them were not swayed or convinced, but you had better believe that some of them were. Jesus' own inner circle would never have become the band of missionaries they did if Jesus had not provided a "taste-and-see," "show-and-tell" world of experience that made their hearts thump again. The boys on the road to Emmaus, after recognizing the post-resurrection Jesus, said, "Were not our hearts burning within us while he talked with us on the road and opened the Scriptures to us?" People long for these experiences where their hearts will burn again. Start by inviting them into some experiences they haven't had before (or for a very long time). The experiences don't have to be hard or push them too far; rather, just enough to have them say or think to themselves, "That was pretty cool; I think I saw God show up."

When Jesus fed the 5,000 and then the 4,000, his disciples didn't do the miracles, but they got to see the young boy bring his basket up and they got to distribute the abundance of food. They had the experience of bending down a few hundred times and looking into the eyes of thankful fathers who were wondering how to feed their kids that day. They got to hear the thanks of the people, and their hearts must have been stirred. As they sat at Levi's table, surrounded by tax collectors and sinners, or as they listened to Jesus speaking with the half-breed Samaritan woman, or as they watched him protect the whore brought to him by the Pharisees, their hearts were challenged to think differently. When they heard Jesus defending their religious blunders for eating grain on the Sabbath or not washing their hands the right way, they began to see their faith as separate and distinct from the religious heritage they could never measure up to. Those who followed Jesus must have lain down at night, stared at the rafters in their hut, and thought, "Man, that was a cool day! Can't wait to see what happens tomorrow."

Whereas a time of *observance* purifies motives, surfaces personal issues, clarifies values, and calls people to something bigger, *preparation* pushes people into an active posture that will connect them with real needs and real people so that their hearts can be reformed after the heart of God.

In Adullam we've worked hard to find ways to give people the time to try God's ways. We created a *TK Primer* that combines spiritual formation practices of Scripture meditation, thoughtful reflection, and prayer with missional habits. Each day they have to dive in with God, but each week provides some experiences that flesh out what they are processing. One week we have them simply throw a party. Another week, they all find things they don't need in their home, sell them on Craigslist, pool the money, and give to people in need. Another week, we simply have them cross the road to connect with a neighbor they've always seen but not related with, walking around the block to meet someone whose head they've only seen while mowing the yard on the other side of the fence. Yet another week, we have them go to a public place where they can watch people, and we ask them to imagine the struggles people may be living with. Then we just ask them to pray for the faces they're looking at.

None of these practices are hard or difficult, but they get people out of their homes or churches where they can imagine and envision God at work. In doing so, their hearts start to beat to the rhythm of God's heart again.

Jesus' preparation style wasn't your typical classroom prep; it was on-the-street training, doing things he was going to ask them to own and initiate on their own after he was gone. His prep was hard at times—they struggled, got angry, wanted to quit, got confused, and self-analyzed—but they grew! They were being spiritually formed, and I believe we must move spiritual formation out into the streets again and give people time to get some wind in their sails before we ask them to do church again.

Second Transition: Public Sending and Blessing

I was speaking to a church in Omaha called Core Community. This church was somewhat of a sister church with Adullam and had taken this process of *preparing* seriously. Just before my message, two couples were introduced to the congregation. One couple had started a missional community, and they were now sending the other couple who had been with them to begin yet another community. I remember thinking at the time how much that communicated to the entire church what the values and hopes were for everyone. The public "sending" of one of their own couples to forge out a new community inspired the congregation far beyond what my sermon would do.

No matter how you view past membership processes, we believe that this next transition, the one between preparation and participation, is the best place to publicly acknowledge a person's intent to follow Christ again. Just as baptism is a huge public encouragement and a witness to the community—a person's intent to follow Christ for the first time—why not provide the same experience to those who are ready to try again? Whether they are a jaded, tapped-out, leery-of-church past follower or a transfer Christian, publicly acknowledging their willingness to go through an intentional but informal process of observance and preparation, and then committing them to embody the missional/incarnational values of the church will mean the world to them as they are prayed for and sent. This is a beautiful time to make use of the biblical precedent of "laying on of hands," and you will find that this experience can often be just as meaningful as baptism was for that individual.

Participation

Participation is exactly what it sounds like. People are now trying and doing. They've been publicly sent after a time of preparation, and now they are learning how to live a naturally incarnational life. Although the bar has been raised to help them get to this point, it's actually okay to lower it a bit as you want to communicate and reinforce that they are a part of grace-filled community in which we never fully perfect this new missional life, but we keep moving ahead. It's critical to communicate this to them because the idea of "trying harder" has generally been a let-down for most people. We often remind them that our goal is not just to get them into an incarnational community so much as to see them learn to live this way intuitively. In the *TK Primer*, our last chapter (p. 171) says it this way:

> So, here we are at the end of our eight weeks together. We'd guess that by now you are beginning to understand the high calling and responsibility of being a missional Christian and incarnationally influencing people around you. But you may also have become aware of the many barriers to living this way, especially as it challenges our own susceptibility to consumerism, materialism, and individualism. Even more, we have the normal obstacles of life: work, health, family, finances, global concerns, pressures, problems, and just plain fatigue. We hope that if you remember anything about this process, you'll focus on the fact that incarnational community can happen anywhere. If you perceive it as one more program you need to add to your already complicated life, you'll never make it. But if you understand this as something more fundamental, that is, something central to who you are, then you may be surprised at what God can do in your life. What we're talking about is really personal transformation. It is the process of developing new habits of life and new concepts of what it means to be "on mission." We have a special name for this process: the Intuitive Life. Intuition is the ability to sense or know without conscious reasoning. Learning to live intuitively is important because life rarely happens in steps, programs, or logical sequences. In fact, most of the time, it just happens. Developing an intuitive, incarnational lifestyle is an organic process and it depends on our willingness to listen and respond to God's direction. For it to emerge, we must learn to trust and lean on faith and the Holy Spirit, being sure that God is faithfully working in and through us.

When Jesus left and told his people that it would be better for them if he went away, he actually meant it! He reminded them that he had modeled what he had taught and had let them experience enough of kingdom life that he could now ask them to take ownership of his mission and lead others to do the same. His global takeover was initiated with just a handful of apprentices, and we're here today because of a chain of grace that began with people who learned to live — not a program or a religious life, but an *intuitive* life. They woke in the morning expecting that God had prepared a fruitful day for them; they reorganized their lives, resources, and relationships so that they could respond to the Spirit's leading; their passion was contagious, transforming, and easily transferred to others who would follow the ways of Jesus.

Participation is just living with no particular goal in mind except faithfulness to Jesus. I met with one community that had actually left a church together because the church experience had lost meaning for them, but they had all stayed together. They read about our story and wanted to process how their community might fit into our network. As I answered their questions on the patio one warm summer evening, one of the girls asked, "I really like the posture of Adullam and how you call everyone to take it seriously and actually die with you, but what does dying look like in real life?"

I said, "It's just living well and being willing to give time, resources, and relationship to people who are looking for what you have. It's opening your home for dinners, inviting sojourning people into your family time, recreation, and hobbies, and into your spiritual community. It's not rocket science or martyrdom at a biblical story level, but you do have to die to your natural bent to live exclusively to yourself. You have to let Christ's mission dictate how you live. It's really about the direction of your life, not a state of perfection. It's serious, but it's also a beautifully whimsical life without legalistic pressure or self-judgment."

After a quiet moment, she asked, "So what would it look like for us to join you?"

"Simply come be with us and participate with us. It's a life, not a program. There are huge hopes for people and our own growth, but participation is just an invitation to stay in the game with Jesus and others who take his call seriously."

Jesus raised the bar on the front end and then lowered it once he had the hearts of people. He let them observe what he did, and then he prepared the sojourners to follow him in death. To those who were willing to carry his load, he taught that his burden was actually quite light. We recommend that you do the same. If you're talking to transfer Christians or a new core group helping you start a new church or jaded recovering saints, be honest with them. Tell them you're not that interested anymore in playing church and that you don't really care if they come or not. Watch as many find another church, but then enjoy the conversations with the few who begin to settle around the waft of your missional calling. Start preparing them, pray over them, send them publicly, and then relax and help them learn to relax. What you've just invited them into is a life ... an intuitive life that will change everything they've ever known about following Jesus.

Third Transition: Commission (and Membership?)

One of our most passionately asked questions is, "What about membership?" The fervor with which the question always comes, shows how deep the issues really are. Essentially, what every leader wants to know is, "How do we get people to commit to a higher level of discipleship? What should these requirements or expectations be? When should this point be?

Traditionally, many tackle these questions with the idea of membership. Yet, for most churches, membership has become empty and meaningless and does not seem to emote authentic enthusiasm or produce the level of transformation we hope it will.

Regardless of our respective styles or modes of church, this third transition is where the answers lie. We believe that the progression toward ownership and then the celebration of someone's intentional partnership is the most valuable transition in the Christian life for any believer, and it should cause us to rethink everything and commit our best effort toward apprenticing every person to this point.

Remember our leadership principle: "To whatever you give your leadership, it will grow." If you give your time to working with your staff to prepare a great weekend church service, you'll probably have one. You meet your staff two or three times, they all are working tirelessly to pull off their individual responsibilities, and the average church probably spends the combined hours of three to eight staff to the tune of 120 hours a week. You should have a great Sunday service if that is your goal.

But according to this principle another option is available to you. If you want to see people go beyond a Sunday service experience and learn to be like Jesus, you will need to give the time you used to give to preparing for that, to this new goal. In other words, if you want your people to someday take ownership over your church's future and partnership in leading and caring for people, you'll need to shift your focus and redirect your time to help them. Our recommendation is that your official training times and coaching of your people need the highest investment in time and energy.

For us, our village training evenings are the best things we do. It's personal, intimate, and focused on the needs and issues they face; if possible it's not done at the church. We put on a huge spread of food, cover their childcare needs, and let them stay as long as they like. We want them to know that our best efforts are given to those who take on the call of leading and caring for others. This simple shift has allowed Matt and me to oversee our entire congregation with only a couple days a week of our time. The people care for each other and engage the culture with the same DNA with which we began Adullam.

Partnership

Partnership, therefore, represents a level of leadership where someone is actually partnering or taking ownership of not only their own growth, but also the growth of others. It can represent your paid staff and your elders, but it also represents any Christian who has positioned his life so that he has the time, resources, and energy to shepherd people. Paul said in Philippians 1:4–5: "In all my prayers for all of you, I always pray with joy because of your partnership in the gospel from the first day until now."

As with any aspect of maturity, partners tend to reveal themselves to you simply through their faithful commitment, giftedness, stability, and the ways they sacrifice for the larger community. Yet we also find that they, too, need to be called out. Most of the best leaders we've had didn't think they really had what we wanted, and it's always a powerful time when you take someone aside and acknowledge (privately and before the community) their natural spiritual authority and influence. For many churches, partnership should really represent everything from the paid staff, to the elders and deacons, and on down to the level of your church membership. Each church addresses these issues differently, but we frequently see that the healthiest churches are those who call as many people as possible to this level.

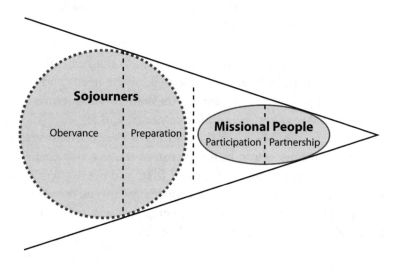

In *The Tangible Kingdom*, we spend a lot of time unpacking a "missional triangle" structure. In that model, we identified two primary groups of people that form the basic substructure of a missional/incarnational community. The first group we call "Missional People." They represent those who have made a commitment to the larger community to live an intentional life and who accept accountability for integrating the DNA of kingdom life (Community/Communion/Mission). The other group we call

"Sojourners," and they represent those who are traveling along with us, deciding if they're going to move toward our community and our God. They're spiritually disoriented God-seekers.

This structure has helped us coach our leaders, but it also helps us keep track of the relational and spiritual steps that people make. In a practical way, it's how we make sure that we're measuring the right things and doing all we can to keep moving people forward. This triangle primarily represented a non-Christian's movement forward in conversion, but you'll notice that as we overlay the same framework over our apprenticeship process, it serves as a great grid for the process of transformation during apprenticeship. Those who are participating and partnering with us fit well in the category of Missional People, and those who are still observing and preparing represent Christians who are still deciding if they really want to grow into the life of any missional church.

As we talk about creating processes that move *non-Christians* toward God and becoming missional people, we need to look at ways of using the same processes to help move *existing Christians*— whether they be jaded, leery, or consumer-oriented — back toward the life of a true disciple or apprentice. We recognize that not every Christian will grow to the level of a partner in the gospel or to the level of a missionary, but every Christians can grow to a level of functional participation. Even if they aren't a full partner, they are still on mission with you.

TRUE AESTHETICISM

About five years ago a personal coach did an assessment on me and told me that I was a true "aesthetic." I laughed because I thought that an aesthetic was one of those monastic guys that sits out in the middle of a field and stares at trees — you know, one of those spiritual formation gurus. He said, "Yes, that's sort of what it means, but a true aesthetic is actually someone who connects with God visually and through one's senses observes beauty in the world. Yes, some people can stare at a lake and feel God's presence; you just happen to have to have a bike underneath you, a rifle on your shoulder with your camo on, or a golf club, but my guess is that is your best time with God."

I couldn't believe what I was hearing. I said, "Yes! I really do connect best with God when I'm with people, engaged in activities outside or after a good sweaty workout. It's like God turns on ideas and thoughts, Scripture comes to mind, and my prayers are the most fervent." This was truly the most freeing revelation I'd had in my entire adult life. I could actually grow closer to God *outside* of a church or a devotional setting. I was given freedom to turn the concept of following Christ into an actual part of my normal life. My spiritual formation could now be "along the way." We hope that this basic framework will also help you help your people toward a holistic formation process that will grab their hearts as they walk with Jesus along the way.

CHAPTER 5

The Big AND: Gathered and Scattered in Perfect Harmony

A significant portion of this chapter is dedicated to the work of Ralph Winter, a missionary scholar whose writings have guided leaders and missionaries around the world. His article entitled "The Two Structures of God's Redemptive Mission" has been formative in our processing and practice of holding the two primary roles of the church in harmonious tension, and we feel it's time for Ralph's work to be infused back into this critical conversation. The text of this address can be viewed at http://pcms-usa.org/articles/The%20Two%20Structures%20 of%20God's%20Redemptive%20Mission.pdf

As PASTORS OF ADULLAM AND MISSIONARIES on staff with Missio, Hugh and I (Matt) live in an unsettled ministry tension. On any given day we're challenged to decide whether our time and energy will be spent tending to the responsibilities of leadership in the church we've started, or giving time helping other churches. The first responsibility keeps us busy with relational ministry, coaching leaders, planning and prepping for the weekly Sunday service, making the coffee, doing administrative tasks, being sure the programs for kids are up and running, preparing sermons, doing the common pastoral counseling and mentoring, and (my personal favorite) — picking up the donuts. Our work through Missio, whose goal is to apprentice a global network of missional leaders for the church, fills our time with writing, developing resources, facilitating training environments, speaking, coaching, networking, and helping other organizations and churches strategize for the future.

We came to Denver as missionaries, not pastors. At the time, we were solely set on the mission of Missio to help all churches, and especially new churches, take a more incarnational stance in the culture. However, alongside this life, we also lived out the principles we taught and Adullam was born. Hugh has already shared the story of how our missionary activity produced a church environment, so rather than replaying the story, suffice it to say that as Adullam grew and transitioned from a hobby, or way of life, to an actual responsibility, we found ourselves wondering if the two worlds were in complete opposition to each other. Would we be forced to pick between the two functions of our ministry? Would the calling to one negate our calling to the other? Many around us suggested that we couldn't do both, but deep down, it felt not only right, but preferable.

While I don't think this dual role is for everyone to the extent that it has been for us, our dilemma pointed us toward some misunderstood issues that do affect every leader. The idea of the AND is that every church can find a balance of both scattering people out for mission while maintaining a biblically meaningful reason to gather together. It sounds like a nice idea but in reality, the tension of the two has been hard for many to navigate. This chapter should help you hold the two together.

In Ralph Winter's article "The Two Structures of God's Redemptive Mission," the author coined two terms — *sodalic* and *modalic*—that we will use to frame what we believe must emerge cohesively if we want to see the evangelical church regain kingdom influence in the world. Through these two terms, Winter introduces the secret to finding the gathered AND scattered balance:

> In order to speak conveniently about the continuing similarities in function, let us now call the synagogue and diocese modalities, and the missionary band and monastery sodalities. Elsewhere I have developed these terms in detail, but briefly, a modality is a structured fellowship in which there is no distinction of sex or age, while a sodality is a structured fellowship in which membership involves an adult second decision beyond modality membership, and is limited by either age or sex or marital status. In this use of these terms, both the denomination and the local congregation are modalities, while a mission agency or a local men's club are sodalities. (p. 6)

Winter shows in this article that the New Testament church formed *modalically* around the idea of a local synagogue, the only difference being that now it was a "Christian" synagogue that included non-Jews. This structure was local in nature, met weekly or even daily for some type of community-based spiritual direction, and it had designated leaders who kept the people together.

Alongside this modality was a unique community completely focused on people outside the traditional gathered setting. He notes that Paul's calling to the Gentiles instigated and modeled the first truly *sodalic* missions community and set in order a partnership of both the gathered and scattered church. Before Paul, Jews were coming to faith and through persecution the church was "on the move," but in most cases they soon settled in a synagogue as a modality. Paul's missionary community was distinct from this and gives us a better picture of the unique sodalic calling.

As time passed, the Christian synagogues were officially recognized by Rome, and they invariably lost their sense of sentness and became "first-decision" communities, where all that was required to be involved was an invitation and a sense of belonging to the local church. These were communities where people just had to decide to believe in Christ to belong. "Second-decision" Pauline missions communities, though, had *another* decision to make, namely, in addition to my first decision to love Christ, will I also make a larger commitment to reach out and interact with those outside the faith?

Although many today think the monastery was a cloistered, separatist, nonmissional environment, Winter brilliantly shows that during the medieval times, as the Roman empire was beginning to erode, it was actually the monasteries that served as sodalic missions communities. They not only renewed the local church structures, but also laid the framework for world evangelization and met many social needs for centuries throughout Europe. While we tend to think of monasteries as local churches, in many instances the monastic movements were known for their "second decision" passion to serve the needs of people around the world in times of crisis and war — even caring for the needs of those dying from diseases and plagues that ravaged entire regions. They were hard-core, second-decision communities that compelled their people to take more serious oaths of service, spiritual commitment, and social action.

Here's a great example from Winter's article.

> Perhaps the most outstanding illustration in the early Medieval period of the importance of the relationship between modality and sodality is the collaboration between Gregory the Great and a man later called Augustine of Canterbury. While Gregory, as the bishop of the diocese of Rome, was the head of a modality, both he and Augustine were the products of monastic houses — a fact which reflects the dominance even then of the sodality pattern of Christian structure. In any case, Gregory called upon his friend Augustine to undertake a major mission to England in order to try to plant a diocesan structure there, where Celtic Christianity had been deeply wounded by the invasion of Saxon warriors from the continent.
>
> As strong as Gregory was in his own diocese, he simply had no structure to call upon to reach out in this intended mission other than the sodality, which at this point in history took the form of a Benedictine monastery. This is why he ended up

asking Augustine and a group of other members of the same monastery to undertake this rather dangerous journey and important mission on his behalf. The purpose of the mission, curiously, was not to extend the Benedictine form of monasticism. The remnant of the Celtic "church" in England was itself a network of sodalities since there were no parish systems in the Celtic area. No, Augustine went to England to establish diocesan Christianity, though he himself was not a diocesan priest. Interestingly enough, the Benedictine "Rule" (way of life) was so attractive that gradually virtually all of the Celtic houses adopted the Benedictine Rule, or Regula (in Latin). (pp. 6–7)

Monastic, second-decision communities not only extended the influence of the church, they also reinvigorated the holistic gospel into the very life of the local church. Winter points out that Luther, who broke away from a monastic structure that had taken on modalic tendencies and unconsciously initiated a sodalic renewal movement, eventually reorganized around modalic diocesan structures. Luther saw the monastic structures as an enemy to his work of reforming the Christian faith and rejected them. The Protestant movement quickly took over some of the more Romanesque control structures, and instead, it was the Pietist movement that played a more sodalic role in the church, emphasizing a high level of commitment.

Eventually, most sodalic renewal movements organize and morph into modalic expressions, but herein lies our call to the church today. The two arms of the church *can* work together! Like a good, honest marriage, where you work through tension for the sake of growth and depth in the relationship, the sodalic and modalic are meant to be together. In fact, they must be together for the church to be whole and expanding in influence.

MODALIC: ONE ARM OF THE CHURCH

Let's now get a little more practical for our situation today. The modalic structure we typically encounter is the local/gathered church. It's a stable environment committed to shepherding, teaching, caring, nurturing, sustaining, and growing us in our faith. It's the "mode" of a structured local church expression. Modalities are mostly concerned with issues related to life "inside" the church, although they can often be outwardly minded, evangelistic, and generous to missions around the world. This mode of church is highly local in nature and places emphasis on public worship, teaching, shepherding, and discipleship. The modalic structure easily includes new people and has few requirements for membership. It's a "first-decision" environment. All that is required to be involved is that you have made or are moving toward a decision to accept Christ as your Savior.

The classic evangelical, Pentecostal, or mainline church generally fits this description. This gathered, institutionally oriented structure has frequently served God's purposes effectively, especially when the culture has come to it for help or assistance. However, when the church either grows too isolated from the culture or secular values invade and water down the church, then the sodalic arm must reengage and call forth a renewal. Just as the Roman church lost spiritual influence on the culture in medieval times, our contemporary churches, with their strong modalic emphasis, have also lost influence in our culture. If you were to ask our unchurched culture today why their spiritual search doesn't lead them naturally to the local church on the corner, they'll often share that they feel the church (modality) is financially self-indulgent, socially cliquish and content to minister to its own people. It's at a time like this that the sodalic arm must step up and begin telling a new story that inspires curiosity with those outside the church.

With the growing chasm between what the culture desires and what the modality-laden church offers, if sodalic, second-decision communities don't soon emerge, the existing, one-armed modalic church will be end up becoming nothing more than a hospital, social/spiritual club, or teaching center. The church will effectively lose its ability to influence the culture.

SODALIC: THE OTHER ARM OF THE CHURCH

The sodalic structure of the modern church tends to be most easily identified by mission agencies (Church Resource Ministries,

Christian Associates, or Greater European Missions), parachurch ministries (Youth For Christ, Campus Crusade, YWAM, Navigators, Young Life), independent evangelistic associations (Billy Graham, Luis Palau Association), church-planting initiatives (Exponential, Missio, Forge Network, A29 Network), and social gospel organizations (World Vision, International Justice Mission). Sodalic ministries can be characterized by words like: sending, missional, new works, movements, apostolic, and networks. Whereas modalic structures tend to focus on caring for those who are already inside the structure, sodalities push toward those on the outside. Modalities prioritize the ninety-nine sheep that are in the barn, while the sodalities push for that one lost sheep. Sodalities see their unique contribution as going where the modalities can't or won't go ... and maybe shouldn't go.

As you read the book of Acts, remember that you are witnessing a story about sodalically gifted leaders like Paul pushing out and starting modalities. His three missionary journeys not only contain a strong sodalic emphasis, but we also get to watch him lay the foundation for these newly born congregations so they can develop some (modalic) stability. Throughout Acts, we see the development of modalic elements in the church: Paul's call to "appoint elders," the Jerusalem Council's deciding the basic requirements for the Gentile converts, and Paul's request for churches to provide financially for the needs of the poor. Many of Paul's New Testament letters are also evidence of his work in establishing the modalic side of the church. Because these biblical stories are "formative," we are also able to witness the tension they often faced trying to establish the balance between these two elements. For example, in 2 Timothy 2:5, Paul exhorts Timothy to "do the work of an evangelist." My personal hunch is that Timothy was more of a pastor/teacher type, but because Paul wasn't around anymore to cover for him, Paul had to ask his protégé, Timothy, to do his best at what wasn't natural for him.

About a year ago, Hugh received an email from one of our younger staff members that had an intentional dig to it: "Maybe if you'd stay closer to home, Adullam would be a little more stable."

It was an email questioning the amount of time Hugh was spending helping other churches. Hugh wisely sent it to me to deal with
so that he wouldn't end up bringing physical harm to the young
man, but I believe it serves to show the tension in all of this. I'd
be willing to bet that there were times when Timothy wanted to
say to Paul, "Hey, Paul, why don't you cool your britches, settle
down, and do the work of a pastor?" There's no such thing as a
pure, perfect ministry (even the ministry of the apostle Paul), and
the early days of our Christian faith clearly reveal that there was
plenty of relational tension. The New Testament book of Acts and
the letters of Paul model a framework for us today as we explore
the dual function of the church.

Hugh and I often talk about how hard it is, as sodalically oriented leaders, to lead the more structured, modalic side of things
at Adullam. Many aspects of pastoral care that come naturally to
other leaders are a constant struggle for the two of us. Hugh has
played the primary pastoral role in Adullam. He teaches most
often, gets the most phone calls from people, and has the most
meetings. If you were to ask people who the pastor of Adullam is,
it's likely they'd say "Hugh." Yet, Hugh is not really a modalically
focused guy. He can pastor and shepherd the people in our church
for a while, but he starts to go cross-eyed and wilt like a flower in
drought if he can't get on a plane and go help someone else. He's
often said, "If I could just be a pastor without preaching, counseling, or pastoring, I'd love it." I tried to fill in some of the modalic
holes that Hugh misses (I'm still in charge of our children's ministry), but I'm even less modalic than Hugh!

Recently, in a strategic planning meeting for Adullam, we
were discussing our discipleship process. As we struggled to define
some of the preparation components, Hugh jumped into the conversation, "If we could just get John to get on mission and lead
some of the guys he hangs out with, everything would be perfect.
What's all the fuss about?" There was a short pause and then we
all started laughing. "Hugh, John is barely a Christian himself.
You just *skipped* the entire discipleship process." Hugh just sighed
and rolled his eyes.

For a leader who tends to focus on the sodalic nature of the church, everyone is a potential leader of a movement. While I'm poking fun at Hugh in this example, it's important to realize that his view and his emphasis are vital to the ongoing movement. Where pastoral staff may be shortsighted in thinking that people just need to reach a certain level of knowledge or complete seminary training before they can be sent on mission, Hugh's perspective is crucial if the church wants to keep the sodalic, sending momentum of the church going forward. But you can also see that if Hugh continues to remain in the lead modalic role, some of the sheep are going to get slaughtered! My guess is that this is the reality that many of you reading this right now face. You have a job that needs to be done, and someone needs to do it, but there's incredible wisdom in knowing which side of the fence you lean toward and trying to find others to fulfill their natural modalic or sodalic calling and functions — before you end up killing someone, least of all, yourself!

TWO ARMS ARE ALWAYS BETTER THAN ONE

When Hugh and I get asked what we think is the main reason that the church has lost influence in the West, our response is not what you may think. Most assume we'll mention the cultural disdain for organized religion, the poor posture of a large majority of Christians, or consumer-oriented ministry. All of these certainly have a part to play, but we think the biggest issue is that we've been trying to reach the world with *half* a church! We've allowed separation to develop between parts of Christ's body that were always intended to work together. Consider what the Scriptures teach about the relationship of gifts within the larger body of Christ:

> For by the grace given me I say to every one of you: Do not think of yourself more highly than you ought, but rather think of yourself with sober judgment, in accordance with the measure of faith God has given you. Just as each of us has one body with many members, and these members do not all have the same function, so in Christ we who are many form one body, and each member belongs to all the others. We have different gifts, according to the grace given us. If a man's gift is prophesying, let him

use it in proportion to his faith. If it is serving, let him serve; if it is teaching, let him teach; if it is encouraging, let him encourage; if it is contributing to the needs of others, let him give generously; if it is leadership, let him govern diligently; if it is showing mercy, let him do it cheerfully. (Rom. 12:3–8)

I realize that most sodalic ministries (what people have termed *parachurch* in the past) have always tried to "plug their fruit into a local church," but over the last five to ten years there has been a massive shift in this approach. In the past, if a Campus Crusade worker led a person to Christ, he or she would find a local modality (church) that would take over the shepherding role with the new convert. Today, most sodalic workers realize that this is just a dead end. Since the conversion process is so relationally based, the parachurch worker who engages the lost and gains spiritual authority in their lives can't just hand the person off to an independent modalic leader. People follow people and communities follow communities, and as a natural missiological necessity many parachurch groups are now sanctioning their staff to start local churches.

This is why the two sides must be linked. Instead of sodalic people trying to hand off the evangelistic fruit to modalic strangers, they should now be functionally a part of the church staff so that the movement from culture to church is more seamless. We don't need Hugh to preach every sermon or be the most shepherding, but it sure helps to have him in the room to help the transition happen.

On the other side, though, many sodalic entities end up creating more tension because they are unwilling to link their work with the idea of church. Interestingly, some of these same agencies have abandoned their aggressive evangelistic tactics and have adopted a more organic, incarnationally community focus—but they fail to allow it to become a "church." Both of these approaches are dead ends. A modalic ministry (like a local church) that is hoping sodalic leaders will go reach people for them and then plug them in, is just as bad as a sodalic leader trying to reach people without a plan to provide modalic ministry for that person if he or she comes to faith.

Another reason that modalic and sodalic must find a way to play under the same roof may sound crass, but it's biblical. To put it bluntly, historically speaking, the modalic funds the sodalic. For the sodalic people to be sent there must be a group or organization that sends them, which tends to involve modalities releasing some of their best leaders, along with significant financial resources to expand the mission.

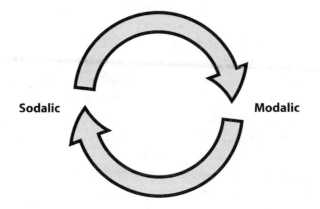

Sodalic   **Modalic**

It's important to realize that the process of growing the AND can begin from either end of the cycle. What matters is that there is an intentional effort at holding the two in tension. When the modalic and sodalic are completely isolated from each other, the church movement as a whole tends to lose its capacity to multiply. A common symptom of this problem is that we often find churches that lack leaders but are rich in resources, while missions agencies and parachurch organizations may have leaders waiting to be sent, but lack the funding to support them. We believe it's time to unite the clans and respond to the call to be God's *balanced* church.

TIME TO THROW WITH THE OPPOSITE HAND

Our guess is that 90 percent of those reading this will be operating in the modalic side of the church and will hopefully find the idea of adding the sodalic invigorating. Any church leader would probably love to throw well with both arms. If you'll allow us to push just a little further, we'd like to suggest that to find that balance, your emphasis must begin to intentionally lean toward the sodalic. It's an understatement to say that in the last eighty years most training, ministry metrics, ministry positions inside the church, seminary education, and peer pressure have been to develop modalic leaders, modalic structures, and modalic skill sets. That's our strong hand. To find balance, our collective response must be to prioritize the weak sodalic arm.

Evidence suggests that the pullback to the modalic in the life of the church will always be stronger than the inclination toward the sodalic. Take, for example, the modern-day church plant movement and how it has developed over the last twenty years. Although every church plant *should* be a sodalic initiative, sadly, in the last two decades, many churches have hived off modalic leaders instead. Typically, these modalic leaders bring along with them about fifty to a hundred modalic followers and end up starting another modality. This happens because we are throwing with one arm. When young leaders grow up doing modalic activities inside a local church, even those who may feel an entrepreneurial call outward tend to reproduce cookie-cutter expressions instead of contextually sensistive *new works*. Inevitably, transfer growth becomes our primary fruit.

As you can see, God's church moves forward, reproduces, and survives from generation to generation because of our sodalic calling. Any sodalic work will eventually turn modalic as a result of the need to disciple and nurture the newcomers to faith, but typically, the missional DNA and fervor wanes and static ministry structures set in. There is really nothing wrong with this process … as long as the sodalic continues to push outward. Practically, this can be accomplished by simply forming our church plant teams, pastoral staff, and elder boards with an equal number of both sodalic- and modalic-oriented leaders. Yes, there will be more tension and lively discussions, but it's all part of the bride working together.

MOVEMENT DYNAMICS OF THE AND

So far we've talked about the two distinct but complementary sides of a balanced church, and we have suggested that every church begin to struggle toward a more integrated ecclesial scenario. Let's now talk about the movement that will naturally occur when the whole church works together.

Then Jesus came to them and said, "All authority in heaven and on earth has been given to me. Therefore go and make disciples of all nations, baptizing them in the name of the Father and of the Son and of the Holy Spirit, and teaching them to obey everything I have commanded you. And surely I am with you always, to the very end of the age." (Matt. 28:18 – 20)

Notice the two sides of the church here in the words of Jesus. There is the sodalic "go" and the modalic "make disciples," and the sodalic "of all nations" and the modalic "teaching them to obey." What most people miss is the big AND right in the middle. It's not surprising! Conjunctions aren't supposed to get a lot of attention. They just hold a sentence together. But as you can see from our discussion to this point, the AND is huge and it holds the key to grasping God's bigger design potential for his church.

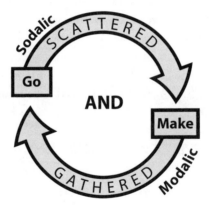

What's great about the AND is that its function can apply to an individual person, a team of people from inside a given church context, or even a team made of people or churches that work together in a city or region. For modern-day examples, we might cite Neil Cole, who models the AND from the organic/micro side of the fence. The sodalic is strong as church is propelled forward in much smaller social contexts anywhere a few committed disciples are together. They expand quickly because a church can meet in a home, a pub, or a beach. The modalic is still there as they learn to gather for teaching, shepherding, discipleship, care, and the like. On the macro side, we could cite A29 network, New Thing Network, Stadia, or Fellowship Bible, which began from larger modalic church environments but quickly and consistently continue to create structure, training, and network alliances to push out and hold together new church plant efforts.

In the middle of the micro or macro exists thousands of smaller modalic expressions (roughly 75 to 350 people) that on the outside look like a normal modalic church, but who continue to send both missional communities out and who plant churches. Austin New Church, founded by Brandon Hatmaker is one example. Starting as a nonprofit social needs–based sodality, a church quickly formed, grew to several hundred, and has now sanctioned several other church plants within fifteen miles. Interestingly, Brandon carries his ordination with a Baptist denomination and received funding from them, but now serves as a missional church plant director for the Free Methodists and receives funding from Hill Country Bible Church to help support other church planters completely unaffiliated with any of the aforementioned denominations. The greater the collaboration, the greater the potential. The more aggressive the partnerships, the more expansive the movement becomes.

THE FOUR PRIMARY FUNCTIONS OF A MOVEMENT
Vision

First, there is the function of vision. This is the ability to cast a picture of God's desired goal for the church or movement beyond where the modality is presently at. Vision is most effective when it comes from a person or team of people who have actually modeled the new way forward and can share from experience instead of from philosophy. For instance, many pastors want to call their congregations to the new "missional" picture, but they are just translating through their sermons and teaching something they are reading during the week at the office. This generally falls flat. Vision is best delivered through sodalic leaders who have been to the promised land and can speak with authoritative confidence, leading people to push further than they think they can go. In many cases, the visionary role is held by those who are both prophetic and evangelistic.

Training
The second function is that of training. Ephesians 4:11 – 13 says:

> It was he who gave some to be apostles, some to be prophets, some to be evangelists, and some to be pastors and teachers, to prepare God's people for works of service, so that the body of Christ may be built up until we all reach unity in the faith and in the knowledge of the Son of God and become mature, attaining to the whole measure of the fullness of Christ.

It's one thing to call the church to something bigger; it's another thing to actually equip them to be able to do it. One distinguishing mark of churches who have the AND is that they are aggressive on training their people.

⇨ Alan Hirsch and Mike Frost, who architected the FORGE missions training network in Australia, created a regional training environment where local pastors and would-be missionaries could not only be inspired by missional concepts, but receive actual training in the practice.

⇨ Neil Cole was key in the architecture of the "Green House" training environment that could be replicated in any city so that organic/house church practitioners could learn together.

⇨ The Acts 29 Network has both church plant and pastoral trainings that are held regionally; it also provides comprehensive online support.

⇨ Hugh and I (Matt) created the MCAP (Missional Church Apprenticeship Practicum), an online collaborative learning grid for incarnational church planters and pastors.

⇨ Bill Hybels created the Willow Creek Association, which has provided a massive array of training that modeled practical ways for leaders to grasp the vision coming from the top.

Fifteen years ago there were only one or two primary training options for church planters. Today, there are hoards of great options.

Again, as you can see, some churches can provide this while others will have to link arms with other churches and sodalically oriented organizations to get the job done. But remember, it won't work if a modalic church team tries to create their own sodalic ministry training. That must be done by those who have actual gifting and experience in expanding out into the culture, and the wisest leaders are those who don't try to reproduce what practitioners have already created to serve the churches in their area. If you don't have everything you need, go find it instead of wasting time trying to produce it yourself.

Systems and Support

The third movement function is systems and support. Simply put, if a church or a movement wants to extend beyond where it currently exists, it will need administrative support, financial support, communication support, and organizational support. Because the ministry of Missio is often perceived to be on the organic/incarnational end of the church spectrum, we often have people ask us whether or not we have structures that hold our decentralized focus together. Many who come into our training environments are philosophically opposed to "structure" because they were either hurt by it or controlled by it in the past. But here's our answer: the more decentralized you are and the larger your vision of multiplication and missional influence, the more organized you're going to have to be! Although pastoring one church is hard, it's actually much more difficult to hold two together, or three, or thirty-five—even if they are each smaller in number.

Some churches decide to centralize secretarial or administrative support to save each individual expression money. Some consolidate their training and intern environments under one roof, while others get most of their financial support from one large modality and then spread it out to those with needs. There are many different ways to configure supporting a movement, but whenever a church decides to decentralize incarnational communities or actual church plants out into the culture, the leaders will have to figure out how to create sufficient time to support, coach, encourage, and protect these sodalically driven initiatives.

The Actual Modality

The last piece of any true movement is the actual modality itself (the local church). As of late it seems to be in vogue to talk about starting movements without any mention of church. Some seek to start movements of discipleship, some evangelistic movements, and some mentoring movements; others will try to start apostolic movements. Although some of these are good auxiliary works, we believe that any movement must ultimately be about the church. The apostle Paul, who lived a decentralized life, living organically and unfettered to one local community, still guided his writing, words, prayers, and actions to start, stabilize, or support a church. If you want to see real missional kingdom movement, you're going to have to develop some type of modalic expression where people are not only brought to Christ, but held together under Christ.

VORTEX

In our story, we often show the movement potential by drawing what we call our "Vortex."

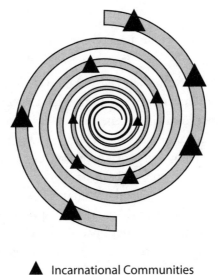

▲ Incarnational Communities

In many ways, the vortex is like a tornado. If you've seen the movie *Twister*, where tractors, cows, cars, and houses are tossed around like basketballs, you've seen the power of a vortex. The vortex gets its power from the incredible rotation created as two seemingly opposing wind forces work together. For the sake of our discussion, these two opposing forces are the sodalic and modalic aspects of church. When all these forces exist inside and are pushing out from the center together, the potential is remarkable!

▲ Incarnational Communities

Most churches have at their center a modalic leader. By nature, a modalic leader tends not to push out from the center, but actually tries to attract toward the center. That's why we often call the typical church "attractional." From the central command, these leaders work at getting everyone and everything to center around church. But a movement is "commandeered" or commanded much differently. As the central command pushes outward from the center, it creates a natural "sucking" response. Whenever we try to encourage churches to send people out to plant new works or suggest that a pastor start small pilots of incarnational communities, we see the angst on his face. "How can I give away money and these people? How will I replace what is lost?" If you've been operating with the understanding that the goal is to pull people in toward the center, these questions are natural. But the bigger reality is that God is the head of the church AND the Lord of the harvest. It's a known statistic that the churches that give away, that take risks, that send out, and that sacrificially push their people out, create vacuums that God fills with even more.

People often ask us, "So if you put most of your eggs in decentralizing people out into incarnational communities, if you give them permission to give their money freely to meet needs in their neighborhood contexts, and if you encourage people to go deeper spiritually, teaching and shepherding each other without such a dependency on you as the pastors, why in the heck would they ever actually come back to a corporate church gathering or give money to the centralized aspect?" My answer is that they are drawn toward the center because the center has empowered them. They simply want to be together and they want to see the influence of their community keep growing.

Because Adullam began with sodalic leadership at the center, we had to draw modalic leaders into our central command. Churches like Christ Community Church (a large multisite congregation of ten thousand people) have a much stronger modalic essence, and they have made the wise decision to create a vortex of kingdom leaders, communities, and congregational gatherings by constantly pushing outward from the center. It doesn't matter whether you begin sodalically and morph modalically, or begin modalically and morph to the sodalic side. The critical issue is that both forces *work together from the center and push out.* The eye of the storm is the most peaceful part of the storm. As the two sides of your church learn together, you will find that your leadership community will be a place of peace and unity.

That's the power of a movement. Though it seems counterintuitive, it's the way God has designed his church to work. It's a faith venture, and only those who have the courage to take risks will experience the exciting results of trusting God. Existing churches need to shake the bushes for some sodalically oriented leaders to be a part of the key leadership circles. Yes, I know, it's easier to get rid of those cantankerously pesky prophets, evangelists, and entrepreneurs; but if you have been operating in the modalic for a long time, there is little hope of change until you find a place of influence for these new giftings to emerge and develop. It's never an issue of being "missional or not missional," "attractive or attractional," "proclamational or incarnational." The real issue is the *degree* to which we represent these qualities. Any church can get in the game, move at its own pace, and still be faithful to God's design for the church.

A massive "morphing" is about to take place in the church. We can choose to learn from our past mistakes, share our best approaches, champion multiple forms, and find our unique contribution in line with the way God has gifted us, either modalically or sodalically. In the next chapter, we'll see how this morphing can happen in the church.

CHAPTER 6

Morph: Transitioning from *Gathered* to *Gathered AND* Scattered

 Hi Hugh, I'm wondering about getting into the MCAP for this fall. Our denomination has decided that they are done with attractional church plants and are willing to let us try a missional church plant, so we're hoping to learn how. Don

I'm not sure how long it is supposed to take, but we're a 20-year-old church and it seems like the more I preach about missional church, the more people I lose. I'm wondering if I should just expect that I may have to restart this whole thing to get there, or if I should leave before I kill the church. Kevin

 Matt, what do you think is the percentage of people I should mentally and emotionally expect to leave our church if I start

moving us away from a programmatic approach we've had for
the last 12 years? Dave

Okay, so we've just set a framework for balancing the gathered, modalic aspects of the church and the scattered, sodalic essence of the church. I don't know of a leader anywhere who wouldn't love to see these two elements come together in their context, but we've left a huge question mark over the issue of *how* to do all this. How can leaders and churches navigate the balance of the AND with as little blood-letting as possible?

So far, we've seen that missionality must be a part of every church and that you can get there from scratch or start moving there from any type, style, or lifecycle of an existing church. Yet we have also learned that there's more at stake than just deciding to dabble in missionality and explore new ideas. In the course of ten years, we've seen a good bit of carnage as a result of moving too fast or too slow, expecting too much, overpromising, under-developing, trying to get everyone on board at the same time, or becoming too much of a purist in one form or another.

I'd like you to hear directly from another pastor looking for wisdom on how to move a modality toward a more sodalic expression:

> Allow me to say a few things regarding the training that Hugh and Matt shared with our congregation. We were a large church (1600–1700 in worship attendance) set on "attrac-tional" modes of ministry … if you build it (programs) they will come. Our senior pastor at the time was honest enough pub-licly and with our staff and we all realized we were simply a cul-de-sac ministry revolving Christians from another church, to ours, and then back to another church eventually.
>
> We brought Matt and Hugh in to give us other options for how we viewed everything. After they trained 1/3 of our adults we realized that it had significantly and systemically shifted our paradigm and our goals, and set us on a path for change in behavior. The missional paradigm captured our people's imagination and also changed the idea of what it meant to be

a Christ-follower as opposed to a committed Bible reader and worship attender. So for us, it was absolutely indispensable as we launched in earnest our pursuit of being a missional church.

Just about the time we had recharted the course and re-equipped the luxury liner cruiseship headed for the Bahamas to become a battleship headed for engagement, our senior pastor confessed a moral failure. It was significant blow and it slowed us back down for over a year, but our people weathered it well because their mindset had already been changed. But I'd be dishonest if I also didn't caution you about some issues. No matter the type of church you lead, you'll have to be ready to address these issues and questions.

First, how will you deal with the natural tension that will come up as people consider any type of systemic change? What about the animosity and/or jealousy that might spring up from the existing membership if the missional/incarnational ministry aspects begin to thrive, which I believe they will? Second, how do you plan to address the distinctively different report cards or evaluations people will have between attractional measurements and missional measurements? Will this cause people to draw lines in the sand? Will this possibly cause a church to split (for heaven's sake no more!!!)? Will this shift cause the existing pastor to look archaic, intentionally unengaged in the community, or irrelevant? Finally, how will the church actively support the new ministry emphasis without it becoming church politics of old (this is usually financially driven)?

John Zivonovic, Senior Pastor, Grace Chapel, Denver, Colorado

This note from Pastor John wonderfully summarizes the issues at stake. We've said that *missional* is for every church. Biblically, it's not an option churches can ignore. We've also pointed out that no church is *purely* missional or *purely* attractional or program based. We need to look at all of this as a continuum of degrees of missionality. This is a key principle to remember as you seek to implement a level of change in your church. If you forget this principle, you'll tend to swing to extremes, expect too much from your people too soon, get frustrated, and/or get yourself fired!

The responsibility of leading change is just part of the job and the calling of church leadership, but it's a complicated task, full of landmines and latent dangers. Each church is a distinct context with unique circumstances and a wide range of leadership giftings, weaknesses, assets, and liabilities that affect how this balance can be attained. Let's address some of the issues that will help you wisely navigate God's call for your unique church.

GIFTING

The first issue you must keep in mind is related to your *gifting*. No church is the same, nor will it be able to change in the same way as another church, because no leader is the same. As we've shared, some leaders are more modalic in gifting, and if the given church has had modalic pastors leading that way for a number of years, it's likely that congregation is used to behaving modalically. Their primary understanding of church is centered around the main gathering, and they are committed to teaching, shepherding, and caring for those inside the ranks. They may have a huge heart for missions and outreach, but like John's church, they will probably be slow to move toward the sodalic.

Other leaders are just the opposite. They are more sodalic in calling and will tend to have congregations that are used to a constant prod outward. Often, this type of church leader has come from sodalically oriented ministries like Young Life, Youth For Christ, or Campus Crusade. In most cases, these congregations are more adaptable and open to change because the leaders have kept them in constant flux.

The gifting of the leader is crucial to assess because it will help you understand the amount of time necessary for change to occur. Adullam was started by two sodalically gifted leaders (on jet fuel)! We've moved six times in four years, changed gatherings four times, and changed how often we gather together—all with pretty positive results. Other churches are more established and just can't bear that same pace of change. A wise leader will take all of this into account.

CALLING

The second issue to be addressed is closely related. It's our *calling*. Calling is often tied to gifting, but not always. In many cases, you'll see that calling generally follows gifting. For instance, Adullam, led by sodalic leaders, has had from its inception a much more "second decision" ethic. We've often scared people away from us because we acted and talked more like a Navy Seal unit than the general civilian population. On the other side, we've seen the "super-shepherds" develop congregations that actually live and breathe caring for people. In both cases, they're healthy because the congregations have lived out of the *gifting and calling* of the leaders. If you happen to be on the extremes, you're probably pretty satisfied your life will be decently content with the pace of change.

But many leaders aren't on the extremes, and they deal with great amounts of tension when they must lead congregational change. A case in point is Pastor John. As Hugh and I have been around this twenty-five-year-old congregation, we've come to see that John is a sodalically gifted and called leader, but he's leading a traditionally modalic structure. When he took over the leadership of the church two years ago, he learned to temper his gifting and calling, adapting in order to lead well. He's able to do this because of the clarity of his calling. He knows that God has asked him to stay inside a structure when he'd much rather start from scratch, but he is called to help the congregation turn closer to a sodalic focus and has long term hopes for their missionary impact.

Many who read this right now are struggling with their calling. You wonder, "Does God want me to leave and fulfill my gifting as a sodalic leader, or is he calling me to remain and use my sodalic orientation to gently effect change?" What you need to hear is that there's no right answer — other than you must hear from God. Your calling will dictate the way you lead, the timing of the change, your posture with the congregation, and the outcome. None of us really knows how our faithfulness to calling will result, and that's why you can't look around and envy what some other pastor is able to do, gifted to do, or wants to do. You must find out what you're supposed to do and then dive in!

For some leaders, sodalic life does sound more exciting. It's often more fluid, "out there," evangelistically driven, and Paulish in lifestyle, while modalic life can seem more mundane, messy, slow, and set in its ways. Keep in mind, however, that both sides of the missional movement have significant tension. The grass really is *not* greener on the other side! If God calls you to stay and serve the existing church, then serve! If God calls you to take a risk and start new works, then do it! But never make the mistake of thinking that one calling is *better* than the other. Both are necessary for God's balanced church to emerge.

Have you ever played a sport that required hitting a ball with a bat, club, or racket? If so, you probably remember how it felt when you hit the ball so perfectly that you barely felt the connection with the ball. This is often referred to as hitting the *sweet spot*. In baseball, understanding the sweet spot experience begins by understanding how the bat works. Every baseball bat has a relatively large area that results in the ball going somewhere, but there's an extremely small spot on the bat that represents the sweet spot. This is where home runs happen. It's that very small spot on the bat where all the vibrations created by striking the ball actually cancel each other out, causing all the energy from the swing to transfer directly to the ball. If you hit the ball too far inside, the energy from the vibrations will go directly into your hands, causing a painful ringing sensation. Hitting the ball off the handle not only hurts like a bee sting, it also results in the ball barely clearing the infield. Conversely, hitting the ball too far toward the end of the bat is like hitting the ball with a mallet, causing a dead thump sound with little power behind it.

I use this metaphor because it illustrates why so many pastors and ministry leaders feel out of place. Some sodalic leaders end up pastoring modalic environments because that's all they thought was available for them. And sometimes modalic leaders end up choosing to serve in a sodalic ministry and end up going home with ringing fingers every day. When we work with missions agencies, which by definition should probably be sodalic, we sometimes drive away shaking our heads because we find that the entire staff and many of the missionaries are modalically gifted. It's like sending a bunch of librarians overseas to minister to a band of wild Vikings. It just doesn't produce much fruit. At other times, sodalic leaders end up as senior pastors and just can't seem to stay out of trouble. If you want to find your sweet spot, you have to know which bat God has given to you and how to swing it.

For example, when I was getting started in ministry, on the front end of my first church plant, I had a denominational leader tell me that my church plant would never work. He went on to describe all the difficulties and barriers that would limit the church from becoming viable. I remember him saying, "You should start your church with a focus on families with young kids because there are some really good programs you can use to get the church off the ground, and then those families can financially support the ministry, and then you can get a building, etc. — a perfect path to successful sustainability." He went on to say that he could even help when we were ready to buy our first building. I remember leaving the conversation struck by how odd his words came across, especially since it was known that I had been establishing relationships with a completely unreached, marginalized group of young people, some of whom were on the streets and none were from strong, stable families.

I left that meeting wondering who would start a church for these people if I didn't do it. The problem was that this denominational leader had filtered his idea of a worthy church approach down to a one-size-fits-all approach that focused on just one core value — being viable enough to have a church building.

To be fair, I can certainly understand the dilemma that many denominational leaders face when deciding how to spend their resources. Getting sustainable church plants going is certainly a valiant effort, but it must also be held in tension with other factors that may be equally as important. I won't deny that starting a church with a strong base of families is a great approach, and many great churches have been started with just this focus. In this case, I had already done all the demographic research and knew the statistics on the city—it was a city with an above-average number of teenagers, single moms, college students, and low-income families, all of which typically lack the capacity to give significantly to a new church start.

If I had my druthers, I might have chosen a different bat—one that had a better chance of paying my full salary! But I had started this ministry by simply building relationships with people whom God had led me to engage. When I first started doing this, I hadn't planned on its developing into a church. I had even looked for other churches to suck up all these young people that I was building relationships with. But among the various churches in the area, I couldn't find a single one that was interested in ministering to this underprivileged segment of the city.

The denominational leader I had talked with had assumed (wrongly) that I was free to choose or change my bat to one that was more viable. What this leader failed to understand was that God had already given me a bat—trading it in just wasn't an option! To be honest, I'm still not sure how I could measure the viability of our ministry during those years in Oregon, but I know that I was faithful to God, our church was obedient to his will, and we understood our context and felt called to be a place of belonging for the people we lived among. Lives were changed, some were transformed, and other people were simply loved with no strings attached. We did the best we could with the bat we were given, and I wouldn't trade it for anything.

CAPACITY

The third thing you need to consider when moving a church toward the sodalic/modalic balance is *capacity*. Capacity represents "what you have to work with." Included in your "stuff" are your financial resources, your building assets, and the highly trained and capable leaders you have. We may all want our churches to change quickly, but you're still bound, to some degree, to the level of resources you have in each of these areas. Early on, Adullam had the fruit of sodalic ministry. We had attracted lots of new Christians as well as several jaded Christians who had been hurt by the church. We were pretty excited by the evangelistic growth we were seeing, but dang if it didn't get a little sticky when these people wanted a little love and compassion from us. Hugh and I have the combined nurturing skills of a chisel and a hammer!

After lamenting this gaping hole in our giftings, we started to pray that God would send shepherds to our church. He answered our prayers and they came—just in time! The people who were being reached through our sodalic gifts really needed some modalic people to care for them and nurture them in faith. Our capacity for this was really low at first and it slowed us down. Many of you may want your church to move in the other direction, toward a more sodalic scattered, incarnational presence, but you first have to pray that God will send these leaders in or figure out how to shake them loose from the inside.

Many church planters I know struggle to hold their people together because they can't find a building anywhere that they can afford. These types of churches also struggle with hiring even the most basic administrative help or pastoral help because they didn't have the funding on the front end. Their *capacity* in the area of financial resources is a significant limitation.

Earlier, Hugh mentioned a resource that we call the *TK Primer,* a booklet that we constructed to help existing churches move their people into sodalic ministry. These have been selling like hotcakes because they are filling a vacuum in the American church. Most churches have not developed a good way of combining spiritual formation with missional living. That's a *capacity* issue. It's one thing to *want* to see your people move forward; it's another to have the calling to actually move them forward. As the leader, you may be gifted to move into this personally, but if you don't have a plan to baby step your people forward, your capacity is limited.

In each of these cases, you will need to do a *capacity* assessment to find the holes that need to be filled before (or at least "as") you lead change. Knowing which bat you are holding will help you assess your calling and gifting, and knowing your capacity will help you have realistic expectations for how far the ball will travel off your bat.

VARIABLES

An issue related to morphing is how and how fast to swing your bat. In other words, how hard should you push people? How quickly should you expect the changes to occur? What's unique about this category is that you can't control it. Like a batter who steps up to the plate, he may know his bat fairly well and have realistic expectations based on his God-given capacity, but now he's facing some ugly dude sixty feet away who is thinking about how to grip the ball so that it will come in an unexpected way. The batter, for this split second, has to adjust to the fact that he is not in control of all that is happening. Don't worry, though! A lot of blokes make it to the Hall of Fame successfully hitting the ball only one-third of the time.

Our culture is a constantly shifting, rapidly changing cornucopia of different viewpoints, people groups, subcultures, and socioeconomic and ethnic divisions in which we try to form and hold together Christ's community, and it provides us with incredibly different contexts for our change process. Even within our individual churches, we have a huge array of cultural differences, theological understandings, traditional expectations, levels of maturity, and understandings of the true purpose of the church. No matter your gifting, calling, or capacity, when you take over the leadership of a church, there are a lot of variables you just don't have any control over.

We might assume that our congregation would love for us to preach on the idea of being a "missional church," but it's amazing how many pastors say it was like preaching *The Gospel of Thomas* or doing a series on *The Shack*. Some people love it, while others will throw rotten fruit at you if they have the chance.

⇨ "Oh, you're now one of those whacko emergent guys, aren't you?"

⇨ "We need to stop telling our people to go hang out with the heathen and just keep preaching the WORD! What are you? A theological toddler!"

⇨ "We can't even pay our own bills or keep our staff taken care of, and now you want us to spend money on blessing the needs of our neighbors? Heck, they don't even want to know God."

⇨ "Why are you all of a sudden talking about being a church and gathering together? I thought we were a missional community!"

⇨ "Why are we doing church services anyway? I thought we weren't going to be a normal church."

I could go on, but you get the point. When you try to keep a balance, you'll end up taking hits from both sides.

The issue of moving a modality toward a sodalic ministry holds some uncontrollable variables, and likewise, moving a sodalic work toward a modalic structure is a good way to pick a fight. So we need to understand what we're up against. Maybe a smart guy from a long time ago can give us some help. Have you ever heard of Isaac Newton? He had some pretty good observations about change, principles that can be translated into the context of leading an organization or church through the morphing process.

Newton's *first law* states that particles with no force acting on them will continue to move without change in the same direction with a constant velocity. This law is often simplified by saying that "a body persists in a state of rest or of uniform motion unless it is acted upon by an external, unbalanced force." Newton's first law is often referred to as the Law of Inertia.

How does this law apply to leading a church through change? To put it simply, the church as it currently exists will continue on its current trajectory, for better or worse, until we begin to intentionally act upon it with new paradigms. So unless leaders move to fundamentally change things, we will continue to see declines in influence in the coming years, just as we've seen over the past decades. The sodalic arm of the church may well be the external, unbalanced force that God will use to initiate the necessary change. Newton's first law gives us a vital reminder that a fruitful future for the church won't just happen; we cannot expect the church to change its path on its own, as if it will absorb the need for a new paradigm and make the necessary changes. It just won't happen. Although the new pressure must be sensitive, well-timed, and in line with our gifting, calling, capacity, and context, it must happen or we're in big trouble. Sensitivity will be needed, permission must be granted, and shepherds will be critical in holding together God's confused saints. But courage, camaraderie, and commitment to kingdom ways of doing church must be pressed upon the existing church.

Practically, then, we suggest creating space for sodalic, entrepreneurial, and risk-taking ventures. Consider inviting business leaders in your church who have started their own companies to a brainstorming session on how to use their collective resources out in the world. Clear the slate for them and say, "I'm assuming you're pretty bored with just going to church; how would you see God using you and your business to bless people outside the church?" Another idea may be to gather a group of parachurch workers in your area together to hear what they are experiencing as they minister to the unchurched. In many cases, these sodalic leaders are not involved in any church. If you create space for them and build a trusted relationship, God may help you find a way for their calling to align with the vision of your church.

Newton's *second law* states that the net force on a particle of constant mass is proportional to the rate of change of its linear momentum: $F = d(mv)/dt$. Obviously, this is a much more complicated formula, but for the purpose of our conversation the basic law can be stated more simply: "Force equals mass times acceleration ($F = ma$)." Applied to the process of morphing a church, this points out a challenging issue that we all experience. The mass of the existing church is so large at this point in the history of Christendom that it will take an enormous amount of force applied in order to initiate accelerating and movement in a new direction.

In a practical sense, this means that we all need to work together. I'm encouraged by evidence that kingdom collaboration is growing exponentially as more and more leaders feel the pain of irrelevance in our changing culture. Never before have we seen so many leaders willing to reach out trans-denominationally to start new works and revive old ones. For instance, as a church planting movement Adullam received financial aid, infrastructure, coaching, or network support from each of the following ministries: Acts 29, Grace Chapel in Denver, The Free Methodist Denomination, Imago Dei and Open Bible Church in Portland, and Core Community in Omaha. And all of this support came without any strings attached!

In addition, none of these ministries really knew one another at the time. They supported us simply out of a kingdom desire to see God move in our city. New networks like "Exponential" now find it easy to get large, self-sustainable networks to meet in the same room to discuss ways to make a bigger impact on the church by working together. Mega-churches are linking arms with organic practitioners and traditional churches are being mentored by both multisite and house church proponents. We hear of the same kinds of cross-denominational, cross-network kingdom collaboration everywhere we go, and we are convinced that only those who seek out this level of partnership will survive in the future. Those who try to prop up their declining ministries, affiliations, denominations, organizations, and individual churches without learning to play nicely with others will end up missing out on what God is doing.

The negative persona of the evangelical subculture, the secular disdain and distrust for organized Christianity, and the growing impact of globalization and the subsequent spiritual confusion form a massive wave that—if it is not met by the force of God's united, incarnationally postured, biblically faithful, and missionally focused church—will wash us over in a white squall.

It's time for a united front of kingdom thinkers, practitioners, and peasants to meet this wave head on. If we keep fighting over the form of our church, if we keep prioritizing our own survival

over our call to send out, and if we remain in our carefully seg-
mented subcultures in the evangelical bubble, we will lose and the
world will lose. Be part of *The Church* instead of limiting your
focus on your own local church. Be willing to link arms with others who share a common vision and passion for your community.
Help those whom you can, while you can. If your denomination
is playing the right game, that's great; but if they're not, choose
to play the right game regardless. If your calling is to help the
immature and weak, then stay behind and make sure they are able
to get in the right boat.

We'll need everyone we can get to stem the tide of irrelevance!
Generating sufficient force (F) to offset the global tidal wave of
Christian irrelevance will require a massive church (m) accelerating (a) to meet it head on. Force = mass x acceleration. To be clear,
getting the church to accelerate in a missional direction will be
difficult, but through united collaboration we develop kingdom
inertia that enables us to apply enough force to revive the church.

Finally, Newton's *third law* states that, "Whenever a particle
A exerts a force on another particle B, B simultaneously exerts a
force on A with the same magnitude in the opposite direction."
The third law is often simplified to say that "for every action
there is an equal and opposite reaction." Even though many of us
in the missional movement are trying with all diligence to move
the existing church to be more balanced between modalic and
sodalic, gathered and scattered, missional and still attractive, we
should certainly expect some push back in the opposite direction.
It's a law of nature—when you push in one direction, you'll feel
a push back in the opposite direction.

In all this "church talk" it's easy for us to get caught up in
the minutia of strategy and methods, arguments and angles. It's
helpful for us to remember that God's balanced church, working
together in mission, is the last thing Satan and his underworld
want to see. There will be kickback from within our churches and
there will be pushback from the forces of darkness. Anyone who
decides to plant one foot firmly in the modalic responsibility of
gathering and caring for God's sheep and the other firmly in the

shifting sodalic soil of new kingdom initiatives out in the world will experience troubles and challenges. Be wise, be strategic, be courageous, be loyal, and be chivalrous—but above all, starting tomorrow, try to begin finding those who need what you have and those who have what you need. Begin dialogue about how you might share, link, support, give away, and get done in your city what you know God wants to see happen. Kingdom mindset is our best form of spiritual warfare, and the more we come together, watch each other's backs, give away freely, and support each other's efforts, the more both the sodalic and the modalic sides win.

CHAPTER 7

To Gather or Not to Gather: Is That the Question?

"PLEASE GOD ... is there any way to do church without church services?"

This was an honest prayer I lobbed up to the cosmic head of the worldwide ecclesia just after I had pulled into the parking lot of a large shopping mall in downtown Portland. It was three hours before one of our Sunday services. It may sound funny, but at the time I was not just throwing up prayers, I was throwing up. Literally. I didn't upchuck every week, but I had come to expect at least four hours of misery leading up to every church gathering, followed by a miserable Monday recovering from what I thought was a colossal failure to produce any change in the lives of people.

I had never enjoyed public speaking. I always felt incredible pressure to lead well, hold people together socially, and have all the programs go well, especially for the children. Add to this the monthly trauma of urban ministry, and I was pretty much a basket case every Sunday. I've had homeless men attack me, urinate on the back pews while preaching, and stand in the back flipping me off for my entire sermon, with both hands. I've had crack addicts interrupt our worship team with their version of *So You Think You Can Dance.* I've rolled around in the church front yard with other chemically altered hostiles, had to pick up 9mm shells off the front porch, and had pigeons dropping guano on my face as I entered the dilapidated church building. I even had a young thief in training come in to steal speakers off our stage while I stood there quietly in the dark praying and practicing my sermon. It's no wonder I made a habit of pulling into the shopping mall parking lot to ask God to take this cup of "church services" away from me.

Your experiences may not be as bad as mine, but after traveling the globe working with pastors, I've learned that many are silently asking the question, "What's the point of gathering God's people together?"

Sometimes their question relates to a feeling that they are "just going through the motions," sometimes it's borne out of frustration over the collective time and money that are spent on providing a place for people to sing and hear sermons, and sometimes it reflects a leader's concern that we are only ministering to the Christian sheep and ignoring the ones outside the fold. It can also be a strategic concern that comes in response to more organic, house church ideals that tend to take the focus off corporate gatherings. Still other times the question comes from tensions that arise due to the personal toll of the weekly grind on a pastor's family and soul. But whatever raises the question, it's always somehow related to whether or not we're really cracking the nut of making real disciples. Does all the work, along with all these resources and all the personal anguish, really produce anything more than an ankle-deep, consumer-oriented Christian?

As we've considered both the identity and the calling of the church, we've proposed that the church must be as much about scattering God's people *out* into the world as it is about gathering them *in* from the world. We now need to address a host of questions that we've heard over and over. So what about the church gathering? What is the purpose for getting God's missional people together? What does God want with regard to our gatherings in any and all forms of church? What ticks him off about our gatherings? What costs are justified in gathering people together? How can gatherings serve our scattering and vice versa? And maybe most important, how can we gather people together without all the consumer baggage that seems to naturally come along with it?

TO GATHER OR NOT TO GATHER

 Hugh, I want to thank you for sharing the story of your church in *The Tangible Kingdom*. I've been reading Hirsch and Frost, Guder, and Newbigin, but I found it hard to move forward until I had a picture of an incarnational church actually becoming a church. Everyone talks about the missional church and incarnational life, but to be honest, I found hope in your story simply because I wasn't sure a bunch of missional people could actually produce an actual … well, church. Then I got even more excited because I found out you guys have real church gatherings. Bill, Texas

 Dear Mr. Halter, I'm encouraged by the story of your church. Is there a way I and my entire staff could come to Denver and check out your church gatherings? We're really intrigued by how missional church people actually do a church service? Kevin, Florida

Hugh, can I ask a quick question. Do you guys believe in sermons? If so, is there a place I can download them to see how you do them? Travis, missional traveler from Turkey.

Most Holy Reverend Hugh Halter, my name is Nnambdi, I oversee a network of churches in Tunisia. We've come across your missional concepts and appreciate your teaching on how communities can take on the incarnational way of Jesus in the world. Many of our leaders are asking, should we still have church assemblies or does that get in the way of missional ways of church? Thank you for your time.

Hi Hugh, I am a house church pastor in Las Vegas and we find much synergy with the unique gathering rhythms of Adullam. How often did you say you gather? We've tried to meet every quarter and lately every month, but it doesn't seem to be enough to keep the relational or vision momentum for us, but I'm afraid to meet every week as it may draw too many people too soon. Any thoughts? Gale

Hugh, I hope you have time to answer this, but I pastor a large church in Nashville. We have four campuses and combined we offer nine services each week. To be honest, I think we do a really good job and people seem genuinely moved by this basic ministry we offer, but I sense that this is as deep as we can take people. As well, I've added up the combined time our staff spends each week preparing for the services as well as the combined financial resources we give to this focus, and I simply can't shake some deep concerns that Jesus may not have spent either on providing an important, but a surface-level ministry. I'd appreciate any wisdom you can give me. I just want to be faithful. Dan

As you read these emails we've gotten over the last few years, you can see that many relate to the idea of a church gathering. As the church is in this time of transition, leaders of every type and ecclesial bent are open to making some radical change and doing some personal renovation. But whenever you start messing with the structure and operation of a faith collective, your biggest questions will be about the dominant ministry, which in most churches is the weekly corporate church service. Although it may strike you as strange for a church to be evaluating whether or not they should even have a standard church service, we think it wise to have an open conversation that can force you to ask the right questions and engage in an honest evaluation of what contributes to the making of a disciple and what may be hindering true discipleship.

Without dropping a myriad of stats on you, the street-level evaluation is clear. The last forty years of Sunday services, biblical sermons, safe childcare, affinity-based small groups, and programs to fit any need are not producing a strain of Christians that have significantly changed the culture. The majority of denominations are in decline, and most honest pastors lament the level of consumerism that exists among their parishioners. We are doing better church services than we have in the past as a result of presentation-enhancing tools; we have time-sensitive programs that are truly helpful for people struggling through life; we have options of doing service times throughout the week so that anyone can attend; and yet we wonder if all our resources may actually be hindering the growth, if growth includes depth of transformation.

So let's jump right in. Should you even have a church gathering? Yes! Once you have two people, you're gathering, baby! There's no smarter, more theological way to say it. If you have two or three people gathering in the name of Jesus, it's a good thing. By sheer logic, if two to three people gathering with Jesus is a good thing, then four to six should be good, and 200–3,000 should be acceptable as well.

Ecclesia (what we translate as *church*) means "the assembled ones." Gathering is inherent in the definition. It is natural for people to find a place to connect with other Jesus followers; it's a natural witness to the world to see people united in a common cause; and it's a helpful way to move people in the same direction, communicate vision, gather resources, augment a parent's spiritual development of their children, find new friends and shepherding help, and share Scripture, sacraments, and worship. So if you're one of those folks who think the church gathering must be discarded and that authentic Christianity doesn't need a church service, you may be fighting the wrong battle or asking the wrong questions. Gathering God's people in large rooms certainly can sometimes make our job of creating disciples more difficult, but it's not the real issue. The bottom line is this: if our smaller, organic expressions "work" in the sense of more and more people coming to Christ and coming on mission, you'll have to navigate their desire to want to be together. You may be tired of the meaningless church services, but they don't *have to be* meaningless.

As much as the corporate church gathering is unavoidable, it is also a natural part of God's story and plan. But as with any good thing, too much of an overemphasis can become a bad thing. As with food, drink, exercise, work, or surfing the internet, moderation is a helpful principle to guide the balance of gathering and scattering. The church service is not inherently a problem, but it can lead to the consumer-oriented faith we've all come to know and lament. Weekly services take a lot of time and resources, and they have the potential of lulling people into a spectator religiosity. This gravity affects mega-churches, micro-churches, and your standard traditional church as well.

It's a refreshing challenge to consider the words of Isaiah the prophet as he expressed God's disdain for the thoughtless religious services of the Israelites:

> "The multitude of your sacrifices—
>   what are they to me?" says the LORD
> "I have more than enough of burnt offerings,
>   of rams and the fat of fattened animals;
> I have no pleasure
>   in the blood of bulls and lambs and goats.
> When you come to appear before me,
>   who has asked this of you,
>   this trampling of my courts?
> Stop bringing meaningless offerings!
>   Your incense is detestable to me.
> New Moons, Sabbaths and convocations—
>   I cannot bear your evil assemblies.
> Your New Moon festivals and your appointed feasts
>   my soul hates.
> They have become a burden to me;
>   I am weary of bearing them.
> When you spread out your hands in prayer,
>   I will hide my eyes from you;

even if you offer many prayers,
  I will not listen.
Your hands are full of blood;
  wash and make yourselves clean.
Take your evil deeds
  out of my sight!
Stop doing wrong,
  learn to do right!
Seek justice,
  encourage the oppressed.
Defend the cause of the fatherless,
  plead the case of the widow." (Isa. 1:11–17)

Or consider the words of Amos the prophet. How much of this critique applies to our contemporary worship services for failing to act in a way consistent with our worship?

"I hate, I despise your religious feasts;
  I cannot stand your assemblies.
Even though you bring me burnt offerings and grain
    offerings,
  I will not accept them.
Though you bring choice fellowship offerings,
  I will have no regard for them.
Away with the noise of your songs!
  I will not listen to the music of your harps.
But let justice roll on like a river,
  righteousness like a never-failing stream!

"Did you bring me sacrifices and offerings
  forty years in the desert, O house of Israel?
You have lifted up the shrine of your king,
    the pedestal of your idols,
    the star of your god—
  which you made for yourselves.
Therefore I will send you into exile beyond Damascus,"
  says the LORD, whose name is God Almighty.
    (Amos 5:21–27)

Wow! What do we do with these words? Rarely do we hear God speak so emotionally and so directly toward his people. And why? Because they were just going through the motions of meeting for sacrifices, prayer, worship, and community. So what's the Halter paraphrase on this one?

> Stop playing church! Don't bother me with your long worship services, prayer gatherings, and self-help classes. I'm not that into your singing and you're mostly doing it for yourself anyway. You've created a God who lets you show up for a weekly service, but you so seldom serve anyone. If you want to get into what I'm into, go help someone! And you who lead ... what are you leading? You are the ones who are afraid to call people to the real deal. I'd love to hear the worship and see the sacrifices if they really meant much, cost much, or were integrated with lives that are transformed. I don't mind my people meeting together, but make it count for something bigger.

Ouch.

A HISTORY OF CHURCH GATHERINGS

As most of us reading this genuinely want our people to move beyond mundane church attendance, it may be helpful give a cursory history of religious gatherings so we can help reorient our folks back to a balanced perspective.

At a simplistic level, spiritual gatherings began with the concept of the altar. Beginning in Genesis, altars were built so that sacrifices could be made to God. Most of the time, God didn't ask the people to build them; it was just a response of thankfulness. Up until the days of King Solomon, most of the altars were created by individuals and villages near their homes. There was no formal, centralized gathering place—just a few stones put together in a pile large enough to make a fire and on which to place an animal. Although altars became a normal and common way for groups of people to worship God, they were never referred to as "holy places." These were just places that demonstrated *human* intentionality toward God. They were most often built while the people were moving from one place to another and weren't what we would consider a stable structure for gathering together.

The next evolutionary step in the concept of gathering was the tent or *tabernacle*. Again, this was less of a fixed location and more like the Popemobile—a place for God's people to meet with God while they were on the move. The tabernacle was the "seat" of the Hebrew spiritual story, and the creation of this location helped God's people by providing a spiritual center for the community, a sacred space. God knew that his people had been stuck in Egypt, that they needed a new spiritual identity after enduring years of Egyptian gods without the opportunity to worship their own God freely. God's directions to Moses as he set up the tabernacle were given to help them maintain a spiritual pulse amidst the dust and dirt of their wanderings and the pull of their past. In the stories of the exodus, you can begin to see a foreshadowing of the elements that make a church gathering authentic—a short-term shade in the desert heat as God's people wandered together in a strange land.

With the installation of kings and the formation of a national identity, spiritual gatherings became more regular and stable. In 1 Chronicles 17:4, King David, out of desperate love for God, expressed that he wanted to build a place for God—a temple of worship. God responded to David:

> "Go and tell my servant David, 'This is what the LORD says: You are not the one to build me a house to dwell in. I have not dwelt in a house from the day I brought Israel up out of Egypt to this day. I have moved from one tent site to another, from one dwelling place to another. Wherever I have moved with all the Israelites, did I ever say to any of their leaders whom I commanded to shepherd my people, "Why have you not built me a house of cedar?" '
>
> "Now then, tell my servant David, 'This is what the LORD Almighty says: I took you from the pasture and from following the flock, to be ruler over my people Israel. I have been with you wherever you have gone.'" (1 Chron. 17:4–8)

Though David did not get the privilege of building and dedicating the temple, God allowed David's son, Solomon, to build him a magnificent place of worship. But Solomon understood from his father David's chronicles and conversations with God that the presence and power of the Holy One of Israel transcended any single location. In 2 Chronicles 6:18 we read: "But will God really dwell with men? The heavens, even the highest heavens, cannot contain you. How much less this house which I have built!"

God's leaders may have understood that God's presence extends beyond a localized building, but the temple still effectively became the center of Israelite religious traditions. The Babylonian captivity, for most Israelites, represented one of the darkest days of the nation's history, not only because they had lost their homeland, but because they had suffered the loss of the temple and now had to figure out how they would maintain their focus on Yahweh without a building. How did the Jewish people respond to this problem? They developed what is called the *synagogue.*

The word "synagogue" simply means a "gathering place." For Jews, these were homes or gardens, or some type of public place, where they could meet for teaching, Sabbath ceremonies, festivals, and worship of God. Although the temple was again rebuilt when the people were restored to the land, at the time of Christ local synagogues ("gathering places") were still operating, although they were held together under the central command of the temple. Later, as Jewish spiritual leadership became integrated with the government and social networks developed, money was readily available for building, and synagogues became more stable structures throughout the cities of Israel and the Roman empire.

Interestingly, synagogues did not have altars, because the Jews still believed that there was only one place where you could lawfully sacrifice to God — the rebuilt temple in Jerusalem, used for worship until the end of the first Jewish revolt in AD 70. The Roman emperor Titus destroyed the temple once again, and since that time the Jews have ceased to offer any sacrifices. But even before it was destroyed, the synagogue had begun to take precedence as a primary gathering place for the spiritual needs of the community. Just as early African-American slave communities creatively formed underground worship houses and makeshift altars, so did these Jewish believers. They were led by a common community instead of separatist clergy, and people found ways to decentralize their worship of God, transitioning from a formal place of worship (the temple) to back alleys, caves, and homes. Whereas the temple-based spirituality had marginalized the layperson out of an integrated spiritual experience by allowing only a few "pros" to handle the duties, synagogues were communities of the common people, and they again sprouted up as spiritual centers for the peasant population in the midst of the Roman empire.

Since the Christian church developed out of a Jewish context where most of the people had spent their time in synagogues—simple places of story, study, prayer, community, remembrance festivals, and Sabbath—this also became the normative pattern for the earliest Christians. One thing was unique, however, within the simple gatherings of the first three hundred years. They were infused with a sense of serious followership. The people were living out a "scattered" existence, and consumerism was a million miles away from their experience.

With the conversion of Emperor Constantine and the formation of a state-run church, however, God's people began transitioning back toward a more building-based spirituality. In many cases, they capitulated to spectator-level worship, becoming mere recipients of the spoken word and religious sacraments. And while monastic communities did give people options for a more fervent, participatory faith, many settled for attendance and adherence to the weekly religious service over full-life apprenticeship in the way of Jesus.

So what do we learn from this (very) brief overview of premodern church gatherings? At a basic level, we should note that God certainly doesn't mind if we have places—physical locations—for worship where we can connect people in our central faith.

He created us and understands our human need for symbols, art, music, beauty, and concrete realities that hold people together. But we also learn from this overview that God's people have sometimes had to struggle through questions of where to gather, how to gather, and what to do when they gather. The "church service" as we know it today is not a God-ordained "must have." Instead, it should be viewed as a contextual option that can be reimagined in fresh ways to keep God's people united together and focused on their unique calling, the *missio dei*.

Whereas the altar, tents, tabernacle, and temple held God's marginalized, on-the-run, wobbling Israelites together, the *ecclesia* of Christ was formed, not as a physical location or building, but as a union of decentralized communities held together by the central life force of the Holy Spirit and the teaching of an apostolic band of leaders who gave direction to the communities. Answering Jesus' call in Matthew 28:19 to "go ... [to] all nations," the church modeled a functional balance between scattering into the culture for the sake of missions and gathering together for the sake of community growth and development. The purpose of the gatherings had morphed, holding in tension the two aspects of God's redemptive mission.

Given this historical backdrop, we'd like to consider some biblical reasons for gathering together in ways that will ensure the proper balance of gathering and scattering.

SURVIVAL

Persecution was the common undertone for the church the first three hundred years, but throughout history, and just as much today, there are places on the globe where Christians get together for survival. Just like the Hells Angels, an LA gang, or a pack of alternative kids who hang out behind the school because they are the only ones who understand each other, so has been the church's story. Whenever the church was on the run, dispersed, under fire, or in the midst of change and challenges, they found strength by gathering together. Regular gatherings of believers gave the followers of Jesus a sense of identity and encouraged them. It also gave them the strength to persevere in their mission. The greater the threat, the greater their need to be together. The more marginal they grew in the surrounding culture, the more meaningful their experience of fellowship. The longer the distance between their face-to-face visits, the more passionate their words were to each other and the more they longed for time together.

We see some of this in the letters of the apostle Paul. Listen to some of his passionate desire to see his friends who are separated from him by time and travel:

> First, I thank my God through Jesus Christ for all of you, because your faith is being reported all over the world. God, whom I serve with my whole heart in preaching the gospel of his Son, is my witness how constantly I remember you in my prayers at all times; and I pray that now at last by God's will the way may be opened for me to come to you.
>
> I long to see you so that I may impart to you some spiritual gift to make you strong—that is, that you and I may be mutually encouraged by each other's faith. I do not want you to be unaware, brothers, that I planned many times to come to you (but have been prevented from doing so until now) in order that I might have a harvest among you, just as I have had among the other Gentiles. (Rom. 1:8–13)

> But now that there is no more place for me to work in these regions, and since I have been longing for many years to see you, I plan to do so when I go to Spain. I hope to visit you while passing through and to have you assist me on my journey there, after I have enjoyed your company for a while. (Rom. 15:23–24)

> But, brothers, when we were torn away from you for a short time (in person, not in thought), out of our intense longing we made every effort to see you. For we wanted to come to you—certainly I, Paul, did, again and again—but Satan stopped us. For what is our hope, our joy, or the crown in which we will glory in the presence of our Lord Jesus when he comes? Is it not you? Indeed, you are our glory and joy. (1 Thess. 2:17–20)

Imagine Paul returning to one of the village churches he had started after a long, hard stint away. He rolls into town after months of conflict, abuse, mistrust, beatings, shipwrecks, imprisonments, mobs, and an untimely snakebite. My guess is that he probably wouldn't have found much solace in his entrance into a church service with five minutes of fellowship by the espresso bar, then a call to worship, followed by teaching and a quick exit out the door. His words in these Scriptures smack of the desire to see his friends, and they clearly express a desire for camaraderie with those who can identify with his active faith. I picture these early church gatherings as big parties with food, celebration, hugs, story sharing, encouragement, and times of meeting new friends. Sure, there were also times of teaching, exhortation, and prayer, but the overwhelming reason people showed up would have been the opportunity to participate in the pull and pulse of communal mission.

In Adullam, we have this really obnoxious bell that I have to ring to get people's attention and to have them move toward the sanctuary from the "donut area." Typically, if our gathering time is at 5:00 p.m., folks come at around 5:05 p.m. and hang out where the coffee and grub is for about twenty-five minutes. Kids run around and people enjoy seeing each other. It always takes three to five rings to actually get any movement, and I sometimes find my neo-Boomer, type A personality coming out when I want to get the show started on time!

All things being equal, though, I've come to understand that this reluctance to stop relating to each other is really a sign of a healthy community. Our people gather to see each other. If you asked Adullamites why they come to church, they will likely never mention my sermons or our worship or our children's church. Although I think these are all pretty good, our folks always mention that they come because of the vision of the church and the people they gather with. This is the primary reason they load the kids up in the van to come to a biweekly gathering. With the off-weekends dedicated to mission and engagement of culture, our folk's first thought on these alternate weekends is relational connection. They simply want to see each other.

I hear your big question coming through. "I see that, Hugh, but we can't manufacture a sense of survival today. We're not persecuted in most cases, so must we wait for a worldwide earthquake or faith-based military conflict to see our people truly come together?" No, the answer is not to hope for difficulty to come on God's people. The answer is to help God's people always find the difficulty that exists in the world. While speaking to four hundred community leaders at Austin Stone Church, they made an announcement just prior to my time. One of their staff said, "This week, Hugh is going to call you to extend your life to your neighbor and neighborhood; next week, we need to call two hundred of you to move to the Middle East to give your lives for this strategic part of the world that needs help."

Apparently six hundred people showed up in consideration of a total life overhaul! This church of six thousand young people in the heart of the Bible Belt show us that any church that calls its people to hard kingdom ventures will simultaneously create a sense of shared struggle, and even among thousands of people, a sense of communal dependence can be created. If two hundred people head to the Middle East, it will take the whole church coming together to make it happen.

In micro-contexts all you need is one person in need to cause God's people to want to come together. When Rena's husband fell back into alcohol abuse, our community wanted to be together to talk about what we could do to help this family.

In any size of church, the key is to help them find enough darkness that their collective light must come together. If the vision of the church is not scary, if it doesn't require everyone to pitch in, if faith is not needed, then folks will stay home and watch the football game.

Here's the bottom line. People get weary of church services when they realize that their participation isn't necessary for it to continue. On the opposite side, if a person feels that they must be there so that God's kingdom work can go on, they will give up anything to gather together. This focus on the outside naturally brings excitement and integrity to gathering together on the inside. Scattering increases the *desire* for gathering.

MEANING

As your church increases its obedience to scatter for i
will see people find what they are really looking for. Yo
a massive value shift going on right now, generationally, which we
believe will force our hand in this direction. Years ago, people
had a high value for loyalty. People would keep working at the
coalmine or auto manufacturing company simply because of their
commitment to the brand, the boss, or the buddies they worked
alongside. Similarly, people would remain in their churches and
under the leadership of certain pastors simply because of their
loyalty to the denomination or church.

Today, people under the age of forty have little of this sense
of loyalty. To some people this may sound discouraging, but I
believe this value of loyalty to an institution is being replaced with
something better. Loyalty sounds great, but staying faithful for
faithfulness sake is what keeps high school students in a relationship with friends who get them in trouble; it's what keeps a wife in
the same house with her abusive husband or a business partner in
company with an embezzler. Loyalty in these ways simply doesn't
make sense. The new value is *meaning*.

My daughters are just entering high school. Cheryl and I have
clearly seen that unless we create an expression of church that
brings meaning to their lives, they simply won't take the initiative now or ownership later. Gone are the days when Dad says, "I
don't care if you don't like church, get in the minivan and keep
quiet." Today, as was the case with the early faith communities,
the gathering of God's people must represent the pulling together
of a unique strain of humans who live larger than the dominant
culture, who earn the respect of those who watch them, and who
provide a much deeper and holistic sense of meaning for their faith.

My daughters love coming to our gatherings to see people they
love and are mentored by, and whom they've come to respect. I
wish I could say they come to hear Dad preach or because our
worship leader is cute, but I can't. They'd easily discard these
things as helpful but not necessary to their growing faith, but
they'd never give up their sense of connectedness to people they
love or the mission they know we're all on together.

Chapter 7

One church we've been associated with is called Austin New Church. Pastored by Brandon and Jen Hatmaker in Austin, Texas, ANC began out of a personal renovation Brandon has been honest enough to share with us. After leaving a megachurch environment, Brandon acknowledged that he really didn't love the poor. To fight his own inner growth issues, he began a nonprofit corporation that linked with other service-oriented ministries to the poor and broken in Austin. As he set out on his journey of renewal, people began to ask if they could join him. This eventually forced Brandon and Jen to acknowledge that a church was forming out of the necessity of holding together people who all wanted to share a common mission to hurting people.

ANC, like Adullam, found that if you try to start a church or grow a church, you often attract people who just want to do "church things"; but if you start with a mission, God will draw people together and church will happen naturally. ANC isn't a church that does mission; it's a mission that has become a church, and the people who now do church together clearly acknowledge that this new way of living is a better ecclesial rhythm than simply adding a church gathering at the end of every week. Again, what brings meaning to your gathering is how well you *scatter*. Jesus gave us the key to helping people find meaning when he said, "Whoever wants to save their life will lose it" (Mark 8:35 TNIV). Corporately, it's the same. If we want people to find meaning in our church gatherings, we must help them to gather for the purposes and people outside the gatherings.

NEW FAMILY

Another reason to gather is connected to the previous ones but is more about the identity of the individual versus the identity of the community. In the West, people are radically individualistic and often painfully insecure and lonely. Whereas the mission of the gospel will challenge these consumeristic tendencies and answer people's internal questions of meaning and commitment, the issue of family will answer their questions of belonging: "As I follow

Christ, will I be a part of a people who will care for me and for whom I can care?"

Read this email from a young gal in our church who was struggling with her faith and commitment to our community:

> As I sat down to think about where to spend Easter, the thought occurred to me that it was more important to be with family and also that, whether I like it or not, you guys are my family — which is kind of a cool thing to realize. You know how it is with family — they don't always understand you, and you don't always like them, but they love you and will always welcome you. That was what Easter felt like. I think I may still hang with the Episcopalians for some liturgy and whatnot, but Adullam are my people. (Wow. It feels really committal to say that ... but also pretty honest.) Alicia

Alicia is with us now because we are her spiritual family.

I received a call from another young man who had come to faith in our community recently. He is a professional lacrosse player, and although he is still trying to figure out how to dance with the God of the universe, he's keenly aware of many friends in his past and present world whose faith he wants to see move forward. He emailed me to ask if I'd contact a young gal in Vail he knew who had shown not only interest in God because of his growing faith, but who also wanted someone to process some questions. I invited her to drive into Denver and called in one of our gals, Laura, to help her process spiritual questions.

During our first talk, she came alive with questions, and it was apparent that God was on the move in her heart and in her life. As we walked out, I put my arm around her and said, "Delia, regardless of where you go with your search, I want you to know that you have a community here in Denver and although you live two hours away, you are a part of our spiritual family." She clasped my arm and said, "I totally feel like I have a home." She now drives two hours from Vail to Denver twice a month and a group of girls go visit her to keep her in the loop.

I'm not sure that many of us can fully understand this level of family, but in Ephesians 2:19 we see the power of pulling together people who had never felt a sense of spiritual family. After a lengthy reminder of how far out relationally and spiritually they were, Paul says, "Consequently you are no longer foreigners and aliens, but fellow citizens with God's people and members of God's household." Paul is reminding people who always felt like "outsiders" that they are now insiders. In a world that is so disintegrated, so lonely, so relationally broken, and so chaotic, it is a powerful thing to provide a place where people not only can find friends, but can find friends with whom to share their search and purpose.

The gut check that we need to keep in mind is that having a church service is not the same as providing a family for people. Although this book is a call to stop bickering over macro vs. micro, incarnational vs. attractional church, we can't be honest without admitting our belief that family is pretty hard to pull off with a thousand people meeting together in a large room once a week. We confess that there is no easy answer for those who already care for more than a few hundred people every week. What's the number where the sense of family is lost during a church gathering? Based on our experience, we think the number is somewhere in the 60 to 120 range. It seems that in this range, people still feel quite connected and known, noticed but not overwhelmed, safe but included.

So what does this mean for the size of our gatherings? For smaller gatherings, it means that you are well suited to have a built-in sense of family, but it is important to be aware that just having eight people in the living room isn't necessarily better if you want to have more for your community than a sense of family. The *missio dei* pushes us all to train and pull our people out of the living room and into a larger social network, giving room for more people to "meet" the family. Just as every family has an extended family with a rich history, your spiritual family has an extended family as well, and if the vision stops at simply providing people a place of belonging, then you're missing the bigger picture. Every nuclear family must also open up their lives to others outside their family of origin. In the same way, every small group, house church, or organic expression of the church needs to be willing to open up and expand. God wants everyone in his family, so you'll have to eventually find a way to hold larger gatherings of communities and people together.

That said, for the larger churches, you'll have to push the other direction. Realize that your large weekly gathering is important, but it really can't deliver that family sense. Your work will be to pilot some small incarnational communities as the substructure of the larger family, as well as some midsize environments in the 60 to 120 range so that the family feel that people get in incarnational communities isn't that much different than the midsize connections. Just because we have "life groups" or "small groups" doesn't mean that we're providing the family-level of connectedness. If you don't have smaller incarnational communities and midsize connection points, those who are presently outside your church margins are not likely to find meaning in the sixty-minute weekly church service.

Related to this issue of forming a sense of authentic family within your church, we have been asked quite a bit about multisite and internet churches where people gather via live feed, video, and a chat room. You might think that we'd completely debunk these experiences where people show up to watch a video of a delayed sermon from a different location. But consider your relationships with some of your closest friends who live far away and to whom you only talk occasionally. For many people, checking in via email, Skype, or an occasional phone call has the ability to give you a sense of belonging with that person. My closest friends live all over the world, and I have found that I don't always need a literal face-to-face interaction with them to have a sense of family.

Can the multisite movement or these relationally disconnected ways of gathering people together lead to some folks being even less committed and more individualistic? Of course they can. But they can also have the ability to draw people closer. The difference is not in the form or the structure, but in how a church moves beyond the sermon download or providing programs for the kids. If a church has mobilized its people to communal experiences of mission, engagement, and blessing in the cities, then coming together to hear certain leaders encourage them or teach via a TV or computer screen can really work, and can even be more cost effective.

The difference is found in the motive for the gathering and what happens before and beyond the gathering. If the gathering propels people toward missional scattering, then it may not matter how we gather or how many people gather together. We are also seeing many multisite expressions that aren't necessarily "mega" in orientation. Some churches actually hold together multiple "midsize" sites of 60 to 120 folks, which not only proliferates a value of scattering, but allows for the gathering to have a sense of family as well.

CHANGE ASSUMPTIONS

I've often mentioned to people that one of my definitions for evangelism is "changing people's assumptions." In our Western context, almost everyone has heard at least one version of the Christian gospel. By what they've seen on TV, heard through the grapevine, or experienced in a church setting, most feel they know what Christianity has to offer, and they aren't showing much interest. When pushed even further as to why they aren't drawn to Christianity, they usually mention a problem with the church as an institution or organization. In other words, they tell us what they think about our formal gatherings and our *churchiness*.

I've always said that people outside the Christian faith often perceive us to be a lot like mice. If you meet just one, they're kind of cute, but if you come into a room full of them, they can really freak you out! So if people's hang-up isn't as much about Christ as it is about the idea of "church," then we have an opportunity to help reshape their opinions by reshaping what our gatherings look and feel like.

I'm not talking so much about rearranging chairs and playing videos. I'm talking about architecting our collective times so that people pick up on the genuine values of our people. Here's an email I sent a friend to this extent:

Hey Dick, I'm sitting here at the opening of the new Whole Foods over by your house. I dropped McKenna off for hockey practice and came over to check this place out. I was going to do a little writing but I've been sitting here fighting back tears as I watch hundreds, and maybe close to a thousand people, walking around in awe over the beautifully laid out store with free samples of incredible food, live music, indoor/outdoor seating, and friendly staff greeting people everywhere. I can't help but picture the church providing such a place of community connection and practical goods. I know we're a long ways from this reality, but it's clear that people are drawn to experiences that unite their senses, and give them a sense of community belonging. To me, it's weird to think that the cost of creating such a kingdom place in the middle of commerce is worth the cash, but as I think about the spiritual vacuum that exists up in this part of town, sometimes I think if I had the dough, I'd spend it on something like this. Just throwing a thought out — I'm still praying for gathering spots that reflect God's passion to unite his people out in the world, instead of extracting them from the neighborhoods and into Christian buildings. People need to see Christ and his people in different environments, different postures, and different practices.

Hope your week goes well. Hugh

Even though Adullam is known for outward-focused communities, we've seen a consistent push by our folks to have their searching friends not only experience localized, neighborhood expressions, but also to experience our larger gatherings. At first, I wondered why we even needed to meet in larger groups, but enough people have said essentially, "Having my friends see how we 'do church' is helping tear down their true assumptions. I want them to meet our people and see how we are together."

What are we like? Well, it's difficult to communicate the intangible aspects of our life together, but I'll give it a try. These are just a few statements that describe what various people have said about our corporate gatherings, and they also serve as a helpful description of the key elements we find in churches that have found a way to gather together without compromising their sending impulse or capitulating to the gravity of consumerism:

⇨ Relationship first, presentation second
⇨ Whimsical
⇨ Everyone's messed up, therefore everyone's safe to be there regardless of their level of faith or doubt
⇨ Communion table is central, intimate, open, participatory, and the glue that holds people together
⇨ Not polished, not excellent, but proficient
⇨ Sermons as story as opposed to abstract teaching
⇨ Children integrated with the adults while augmented with simple programs
⇨ Outside at least every eight weeks at a park (probably won't work in Iceland in December)
⇨ Food, lots of food!
⇨ Simple worship without any hype or pretense
⇨ Leaders who lead through vision and hold the community to higher purposes
⇨ Orderly, but everyone feels safe to raise a hand, share a thought, or ask a question
⇨ Sacrilegious, but reverent
⇨ No "greeters" but everyone friendly
⇨ No offering but people give
⇨ No altar calls but people come as part of their conversion process.
⇨ No service teams but everyone lends a hand

Don't take our story as a prescription for your story (especially that no offering part), but we want to note that as we observe other churches with similar ethics of gathering and scattering, they all mention similar traits that emerge in their gathering times. We do what we do as a response to what we know the converting culture needs to see.

Each church must honestly evaluate how well their gathering as a church links with their scattering. Many churches and their people say, "Uh ... actually I don't think bringing my friends to our church service would actually help their growth, and in fact it would hurt." But others can't wait for their friends to experience the larger corporate experiences. If you're in the first group, you'll have to address why your corporate gatherings are a turn-off and be willing to adjust. Some may not be able to adjust, and in those cases you can use the misery of your people to propel new church planting efforts.

CHILDREN

The question we are most often asked regarding all that we've written about incarnational community is: "What do you do with children?" Obviously, this is an important question as people who have been used to taking their kids to church, dropping them off, and then repeating the process every seven days are now wondering what will happen to the spiritual life of their children if they change their church experience. They're also processing how they can maintain some sense of sanity now that they aren't able to drop their kids off once a week!

I do find it interesting that as Western Christians we so quickly panic when we have to think beyond programmatic ministry models. In other cultural contexts, if you asked a Hindu, Buddhist, or a Christian what they do with their kids during religious services, you'd probably get a weird response like, "You include them." This really shows how *church* has dis-integrated our experience to the point where we don't think we as big people can grow with God if our children are with us.

You know the real story if you've read the Bible. Parents passed down their active faith to their children by including them in the life of the community. Everything was integrated. They didn't need programs because all the parents prioritized the passing on of the story of faith, the passion of faith, and public commitment to the community. Nowadays, many children and teens don't have a functional family in which to learn and incorporate God's story. Many Christian parents have never learned how to lead their own children. Thus, some level of help offered by the church is warranted and necessary. Yet we can't gloss over the fact that much of what we provide isn't really for these situations. Instead, we communicate that our church gatherings are where your kids will get their primary spiritual education and in turn the consumer cycle begins again. Discipleship of the whole family must begin by handing back the primary "teacher" role to the parents. Church-based ministry should augment—not replace—what they receive at home.

My girls have never attended a youth group or experienced an age-based programmed children's ministry, except as toddlers in our first church plant. Yes, there have been times where my wife and I have wondered if we were short-sheeting our kids, but now that they are in high school, we're deeply grateful for the wide range of experiences they've had with *church*. If you were to ask them, "So what do you remember about church?" they'd probably mention many gatherings in our home, parties, holiday feasts that always included many people that didn't have a home to go to, Bible studies where they would sit on the couch with the big people and participate as part of the group, large all-day gatherings at three or four parks, meeting in community centers, meeting in old churches, helping with the nursery kids, serving people, taking gifts to people, praying around our kitchen spontaneously with larger groups, praying in church services, being mentored by older girls who had become like family to us, singing, and babysitting kids for other communities so they could have "big people" time. They've had Sundays going to church and Sundays being the church.

Over the course of their lives, my children may not be able to think of just one thing when the word "church" comes to mind, and I believe that will naturally cause them to want to replicate and reproduce the same active church life they grew up in. Now as they enter mid-high school years, I'm encouraging them to be a part of a ministry that is focused on missional life to their non-Christian friends like YFC or Young Life. I don't see these as parachurch organizations, but as being more in line with the sodalic arm of the church. I think that being involved with these organizations will strengthen their understanding of their own missional call.

All parents want the best for their kids, but as we mentioned in the chapter on consumerism, God's highest goal for our children isn't to keep them busy and safe. Our role as stewards over the spiritual life and legacy of our kids is to model a holistic life of apprenticeship under Jesus—to invite them and include them in as much as you can and to trust that God will grow them, protect them, and use them to change the world. This certainly can include children's education during our gathering times, but it must include much more. Children will follow what they've seen us do. If they see us go to church and live a typical, normal life, that's what they'll think being a Christian is all about. But if they see their parents actually live out the gospel—community, sacrifice, inclusiveness with everyone, and mission to the poor and needy—they will follow suit.

The more decentralized and organic your church rhythms, the more creative and intentional your people will need to be with each other and for each other, with and for their children.

WHAT ABOUT THE SERMON AND WORSHIP?

You will notice that throughout this book we haven't mentioned much about what you might call "worship." It's assumed! Everywhere people are gathered there is an opportunity to expand our notion of worship. Yes, singing together is still a meaningful experience for a large section of the existing church population, but you'll find that as your church reaches deeper and deeper into the culture, this experience will be perceived as weird for some and nice for others, but surely not the most important reason they gather in a church service. Use this as an opportunity to expand their understanding of worship forms as well as ways of participating in worship as a lifestyle.

These transitions toward a more balanced approach that encourages the scattering of the church in missional endeavors will also help to expand our view of the teaching/preaching ministry. We all know that if there's anything that the collective Western church has done well, it's that we preach good, biblical sermons millions of times every week to people who love God's Word. Sermons have been an important part of our spiritual formation and will continue to fill that role, but we must also face the fact that even though we preach well, our focus on preaching as the *main thing* has not produced the level of discipleship we had hoped it would. Even more, our priority for pulpit-centered Christianity may actually be one of the most consumer-oriented aspects of evangelicalism today. Just as we must reimagine the church gathering, we must also have the courage to reimagine how we teach our people the Scriptures.

This may sound a bit crass, but here's the real deal: most churches spend the majority of their staff time and financial resources paying for and preparing to deliver a sixty-minute program, which prioritizes preaching. All of this, even though within twenty minutes, most adults have forgotten 95 percent of what they just heard. If the church were like a business, that would be like putting 90 percent of your investment portfolio into a product that has not produced growth for the past forty years. It's like the Houston Rockets giving Yao Ming 90 percent of the team's salary budget and running 90 percent of the plays through him, making him responsible for shooting 90 percent of the shots and still expecting the team to win. Or it's like trying to get your car to drive nicely when you only have one of the four wheels with an actual tire on it.

I think you get the point. We need to make intentional investment choices, and yes, you still need a 7 ft. 6 in. Chinese center on your basketball team, and you'll certainly need that one good tire on your car. These are all important, but you'll need a lot more than *just* those things. None of them can carry the load by themselves. The church service with a sermon has and always will be necessary and helpful, but if used as the main way of making missional disciples, it falls far short.

Ephesians 4:11–13 gives us freedom in this regard when it suggests that "prophets, evangelists, and pastors and teachers have been given to equip the body to do the work." I'm not sure how we took this to mean that God gives us preachers to keep us happy and fed as followers. These gifts (or offices of ministry) are given to help train church members do the actual work of evangelism, pastoring, and teaching. Imagine what would happen if the average pastor/teacher who gives 25 to 30 hours a week to preparing a sermon actually gave 25 to 30 hours a week to teaching people how to teach other people the Scriptures? It would so outpace the amount of biblical discipleship and scriptural knowledge in our people that we'd never go back to the old model!

Hopefully this discussion on the purpose and nature of a gathering has helped you think through your own context. Let me close with a few final encouragements and suggestions that may help you ensure that your gatherings serve the scattered missional call of your church as well as creating an environment where your scattered saints actually want to gather.

Pointer 1. The gathering should be a different experience from what people get in their scattering. What makes church eventually lose its allure is that it is always about the same old things: we have Christian fellowship, Bible teaching, and worship in both our main gatherings and in our small groups (which include the same people too). The only difference is that there are more people in the main gathering. Eventually, every person asks, "What am I doing this for again?"

We've tried to point out that people are looking for a much bigger story—a story where they're tested and where they get to participate, live by faith, and learn to orient their already overburdened lives around the gospel mission of Jesus. If our churches provide multiple experiences where people feel that they are growing and get to taste and feel something different, they'll love everything about the church. But if they know that showing up anywhere will only add to the same experiences they've always had, with the same kind of people, they'll eventually join the Church of the Jaded and leave.

If your scattered rhythms are about mission, helping people, relational connection, belonging environments, and on the street discipleship, your gathering should provide something different from these experiences. Each church does tend toward a handful of these, so all that's needed is an assessment of what we do well at the gathering and then make sure we help our scattered communities do something different.

Pointer 2. The gathering should not pander to consumeristic tendencies but should be a place to call people into a bigger story of giving their life away.

Hugh, I've been to Adullam for about a year now. Yesterday, during and after Lou's talk, I felt like I understood things a little better. And then going to the park afterwards to play volleyball with Laura, Sean and some others, it hit me some more. Adullam is best defined by what its people are actively doing in their community. By just showing up on Sunday and trying to find your fit, the meaning of our community becomes more and more vague. And I think that's where some people get hung-up and frustrated because they can't find such internal structure to lead them to their purpose. Adullam's people need to be active with the nonbelievers in their lives in order to discover what we are about. I like that things remain loose and sort of intangible within our "church." It forces people to make fruit outside our own walls, where Christ is trying to lead us. I'm glad I haven't gotten involved, per se in the usual ways Christians find fulfillment in their churches. I've taken time to learn what Adullam is about and I finally find myself in agreement with it. Thanks, Sue.

Sue began to understand the meaning of both the gathering and our decentralized scattering by witnessing both happen on the same day, but in different venues. Each aspect served the other.

Pointer 3. The gathering should be the most pliable, flexible, and adjustable aspect of the church. In Matthew 9, we are reminded of a ministry principle we can easily lose sight of, especially when we consider the last several decades of the church in the West:

> No one sews a patch of unshrunk cloth on an old garment, for the patch will pull away from the garment, making the tear worse. Neither do people pour new wine into old wineskins. If they do, the skins will burst; the wine will run out, and the wineskins will be ruined. No, they pour new wine into new wineskins, and both are preserved. (Matt. 9:16)

Entire commentaries have been written on this passage, so forgive our simplistic synopsis. Essentially, wine is the real deal—the product, the thing people want to taste, enjoy, and experience. I'd call it "the gospel"—the good news of all the hundreds of unique and beautifully accessible aspects of the kingdom of God. To God, the wine is the most important thing. Like any master winemaker, great care has been given from the preparation of the soil, to the planting of the correct vines, to vine maintenance, to harvesting, and then to storage. Any step along the way that isn't carefully thought through leaves you with something nobody wants. Have you ever noticed that most wine bottles tell the consumer what the wine was held in, such as "Oak casks," "Sherry casks," "Double barreled"? They do this because people know that what the wine is held in is critical to the flavor of the wine.

When Jesus is warning about old wineskins, he's letting us know that he really cares about the wine—the real gospel of the kingdom—and that kingdom people should "taste good" to the world he died for. He understands that the wineskin is the form of church or ecclesial structures and rhythms that people come to associate with the wine. The point is so simple a third grader can figure it out. If your holding tank for the wine is bad, inappropriate, outdated, insensitive, or overfocused on the wrong things, or if it takes the focus away from the wine and taints its purity, it needs a new vessel, a new covering, a new "thing" to hold the wine better.

When I read this, I don't get the impression that the guy who recognizes his wineskin is crumbling will angrily and hastily pour the wine out and then throw the old wineskin against a big oak tree, shouting profanities at it. He recognizes that the wineskin isn't bad or evil. It just shows that there is a problem. Either time, climate change, heat, poor craftsmanship, or whatever rendered the holding tank less than desirable and so he probably mutters to himself, "Oops, there goes another bad vessel." He then finds a more suitable one for his precious wine to be poured back into. I think that's a better way to look at our church gatherings—constant evaluation, but then a more emotionless and practical willingness to make sure it is still working well for the wine.

If our gatherings communicate to the people inside and outside that the main thing about being a Christian is that you go to a weekly church service and we're going to keep doing them as we always have, our wineskins are about to burst! Worse, if we think the world is silly enough to buy the wine simply because we spruce up the bottle a bit, or hive off the same bottle to another growing suburb to start a new bottle that looks and feels like the old bottle, we're in trouble. People outside the church aren't even looking for a bottle. They intuitively know that our wine tastes bad and that our bottles aren't much better. They're looking for new wine—something they can taste through God's people scattering among them.

If our gatherings can take on a fresh, soft, pliable partnership with the larger story that's being told through the scattered, incarnational life of our people and their communities, our wineskins can easily be adjusted and people will be drawn to both.

Pointer 4. Gather in a way that makes them want to GO. While traveling to Dallas for a leaders' meeting, Matt and I reflected on a metaphor developed in Reggie McNeals's book *Missional Renaissance* (Horboken, NJ: Jossey–Bass, 2009) that helped us picture how a church can find balance between the gathered and scattered essence of every church. Imagine an airport trying to be so nice, provisional, and self-sustaining that people never wanted to leave. I've been in many airports and some have some pretty unique draws. Portland has great coffee, live music, and really accessible car rental. Orlando has a lively ocean feel. San Francisco has the classic Bart train that takes you downtown without any hassles. Vancouver, British Columbia, has great sushi. Each of these is a draw card, but none of them is so nice that I'd seriously consider staying there rather than heading to a hotel or on to my destination.

Imagine, though, if an airport tried really, really hard to keep you there. It just doesn't make any sense. That's not what airports are for. They aren't destinations. They are gathering and sending places that happen to have some unique and helpful functions. Our church gatherings must begin to take this analogy seriously and find meaningful ways to provide corporate experiences that naturally propel people outward while providing just enough to make their seven-day journey through life meaningful, communal, and spiritual.

The church is beautiful when she is sent, and the sent church will always be beautiful when she gathers in a way that highlights and complements her sending nature.

CHAPTER 8

Legacy: Live as if You're Really Dying

"EVERYBODY WANTS TO GO TO HEAVEN, but nobody wants to die." Joe Lewis

"Death is more universal than life; everyone dies, but not everyone lives." A. Sachs

"As a well-spent day brings happy sleep, so life well used brings happy death." Leonardo da Vinci

"Millions long for immortality who do not know what to do with themselves on a rainy Sunday afternoon." Susan Ertz

"Where life is more terrible than death, it is then the truest valor to dare to live." Sir Thomas Browne

"For three days after death hair and fingernails continue to grow but phone calls taper off." Johnny Carson

I'm writing this chapter on Memorial Day. As the sun comes up over the lake, I realize that my children will wake up in a few hours and enjoy a day off from school with friends. We'll do some landscaping on a beautiful new patio we just had installed, we'll hang with our children and probably throw some brats on the barby with some friends to close out the day. Sometime during the day, I'll try to remember many people who have given their life so that I can enjoy mine. That's what Memorial Day is all about.

Although it seems hard to give this day the heartfelt focus it deserves, once you really stop to ponder the honorable decisions people made in critical moments, it's impossible not to be inspired. There's nothing that grabs a person by the throat more than reflecting on a great death, especially if their passing was done intentionally, allowing someone else to live.

I could fill a book with famous people we've all heard about, but in my last ten years of life my mind quickly remembers hundreds of firemen who went back into the Twin Towers on 9/11, the men who stormed the pilots' cabin attempting to thwart another terrorist attack on Flight 93, or Pat Tillman, who left a lucrative professional football career to fight and die in Iraq.

Dying well doesn't have to be dramatic to be impressive. Consider those who have died with dignity and who have left a legacy that benefited others: the godly farmer in Iowa who worked seventy-plus years in the fields, pinched every penny to save small amounts of money every month so he could hand down the farm to his sons; the parents who gave up a posh retirement of golfing, time shares, and fancy cars in place of simple living, downsizing, and even working longer in their job so that they could support a new church, a missionary, or coach Little League and volunteer to tutor and mentor at-risk youth.

As we close this book, we've saved what we feel may be the most important call for all of God's leaders: the call of dying well and leaving a legacy. Just as the thousands of people who have died in honor of defending our country, there are just as many or even more who have given their lives for the sake of the gospel and the church. Though we may not often think about it, the soft road on which most Western evangelicals now build their ministries was tilled by hundreds of thousands of men and women who became as a grain of wheat and died so that new life could be born.

This is without a doubt a time the church must look out and push out from the center; it's a time for collaboration and partnership, faith, and faithfulness. But it is also a time for many to die and die well.

In the past, if every pastor just tried to plant a single church over twenty years, it would have been considered a good goal. Today, we have to think of developing, deploying, providing for, and prophetically calling out hundreds of leaders just to make a dent forward. And that's what we need for each city. Here in Denver alone, there are around 800,000 people between the ages of 18 and 35 who don't go to church. This means that we need 8,000 new church leaders this week, just to missionize one demographic of our town. Like the quiet before a storm or like the eerie outward move of water to the ocean just before a tidal wave gathers force to wreak havoc on unsuspecting tourists, America (and anywhere in the West, for that matter) has found itself in that awkwardly quiet, but subtly dangerous vacuum of leadership.

There's more than one reason we're to blame for this lack of laborers, but whenever there's a shortage of leaders, the blame must ultimately fall on the present leadership. Maybe we've not recognized how many more we need. More than likely we ourselves have never been taught the value of leadership development, and we simply don't know how to mentor the next generation. Maybe we've lost sight of the younger generations because we've been in a constant state of desperation just trying to survive ourselves. Maybe we think we actually have nothing to give them. Maybe we have forgotten that it's God who builds the church — not us — and we just haven't learned to step aside and get out of the way.

There are thousands of forty- to sixty-year-old pastors and denominational leaders caught in the crosshairs, trying to maintain their livelihood while reaching the present generation. That's why we need to stop and consider our legacy: what will be left when you die and how you can prepare today's leaders to die well. Now, like never before, is the time for leaders to reconsider the call of legacy and begin living every day as if they are dying tomorrow.

You've probably heard the country music song by Tim McGraw that tells the story of a forty-year-old man living a normal life until the doctor unexpectedly tells him that he is terminally ill. The man decides to really start living with the knowledge of his impending demise: so "I went skydiving, I went Rocky Mountain climbing, I went 2.7 seconds on a bull named FuManchu …" I'm not a big country music fan, but it does make you stop and wonder: how might we live differently if our mortality, the end of our ministry, or the closure of our church was more an impending reality.

What would change in your life if you really believed that Jesus was going to call the game in forty to sixty years and come back for his bride? My guess is that you probably wouldn't choose to waste your time riding bulls or skydiving. If today's leaders really understood what was at stake and the legacy they were leaving for their children and future generations, I think we'd all be desperate to spend our very best resources and time digging up, diving in with, and deploying as many gifted young men and women into the harvest as we could.

GIVING PERMISSION TO DIE

A few months ago I was back in Portland visiting my family. I was doing what I affectionately call "the institutional loop." I first visit my mother who is in an Alzheimer's care home, then go to see my older sister who lives with chemical schizophrenia in another care facility, then I'm off to see my Grandma Marie in a Catholic Care Home, and finally I visit my Gramma Mo in an assisted living high rise. I always leave Mo for the end because she's so funny and it sort of pulls me up from the blues of doing the loop. She has an incredible sense of humor and her hair looks exactly like Ace Ventura's.

On this particular trip, I entered her 200-square-foot room steeped with the smell of Mentholatum and noticed two nurses rubbing her back. She was sitting painfully on a chair, supporting herself with shaky arms. I sat gently beside her and before I could even say, "How you doing, Grams?" she looked up, laughed loudly, and said, "Well finally … I've been waiting for ya. I'm ready to go, Hugh Tommy."

The two young nurses just smiled thinking that Mo wanted to go down and get a piece a pie or something, but I knew what she really meant. You see, in the Halter family folklore, there is a story of Mo sitting beside her sister Naomi, who was dying in a hospital. Naomi called Mo in and told her, "Mo, I'm ready to go."

Mo replied back, "Well, go on then."

Five seconds later, Naomi was gone—dead. So when Mo said the same thing to me, I literally expected her to keel over right there on the spot! I gathered myself like a linebacker getting ready for the next run up the middle, and said, "Well, go ahead, Mo, I've got you covered down here." Then I braced myself for Mo to slump down in my lap. She just looked down for about ten really long seconds, took a huge deep breath, and said, "Well, I guess I have to stick around a little longer." Ahhhggg.

For the sake of the story, I wish I could tell you she floated off into the heavenlies, but she's still kicking (as of the writing of this book)! But I think the metaphor still works. My point is that people need permission to go. We're not all there yet, but one of the greatest moments many of us will face will be to know that we've done the best we can do and now we get to bless those who will hold down the fort when we leave. Mo was a little ticked that she didn't get to go on that visit, but she still gave me a five dollar bill as she always did, gave me a kiss, and said, "See ya next time, H. T." I left that time, as I always do, inspired by her life, blown away by her generosity (20 percent of her monthly budget), and soberly hoping that someday I'll be able to carry on the legacy she's given to me.

The other option left to us is to die as my mother likely will. Although she was once one of the most sacrificial, giving, loving, and generous people I've ever met, as soon as her mind left through dementia—she left. Now she exists physically, but that's about it. She can't offer help to anyone, she shows no emotion or ability to communicate, she's not productive at any level, and there's no realistic hope of her life improving. Whereas our love for her and her massive worth as my mother compels me to dignify her life by keeping her alive as long as I can, the church certainly isn't dignified by living on life support. Churches have the option of choosing the kind of legacy that they will pass down to coming generations, if any.

The church of Jesus Christ is eternal and lives on forever, but the wineskins of our individual localized expressions of the church and the tenure of our time in leadership do not. We all need to hear this as a warning, but also to recognize it as a marvelous opportunity—a gracious permission slip to begin taking steps to make the handoff. Like my mother, who was stricken quickly with dementia, some churches will not be able to plan for a "good exit." The end will come suddenly and the death will not seem dignified, meaningful, or inspirational. So for those of us who still have our wits about us, we need to realize what a blessing we have to actually look forward to and make plans for a great ending to our ministries and our lives, and more importantly, those who will carry the torch forward.

IT AIN'T KANSAS ANYMORE

Wherever I get asked to speak, I always enjoy walking the hallways of the churches I visit to view the historical photos. Many churches have really cool, old retro black-and-white pictures of all the pastors who faithfully served with a little gold label underneath that gives the length and years of their tenure. Right beside are classic photos of the church's history. There's usually a picture of the building just after it was built as well as a picture of the first congregation standing straight-jawed in front of the main step.

One thing is sure, back in the day when churches began, they planned on staying awhile. Their buildings all had chiseled stone engravings with the date the church was "established." And as new congregations were born, everyone knew which had been around the longest (First Baptist, Second Baptist, and Third Baptist). But we aren't in Kansas anymore. We now live in an era of such rapid change and social shifting that it's just not wise, prudent, accurate, or practical to think that our churches will be around all that long. In days gone by, people stayed in the same city most of their lives, maybe moving once or twice. Our communities were stable and our churches could maintain a vibrant life for at least forty years—if not longer. Today, however, most people move eight to ten times in their life, maintaining residence in a single location for an average of three to seven years. In metro Denver, one-third of the entire resident population moves every year!

Just like college-based ministries, which have had to accept the painful fact that their congregation completely turns over every four years, most of our churches now feel this massive flux. Establishing a self-sustaining faith community is almost a miracle; maintaining and growing disciples is even harder. Congregational death is not just a reality we will have to deal with eighty years and sixteen pastors down the road. It may be something you'll need to face much sooner than you expect . . . and that's okay.

Am I saying that we should just throw in the towel and give up? Let me ask you this: if you knew that your church would only last ten years, would you bother starting it? Would you work hard and sacrifice all you have if you knew that you might have to begin again someday? If your church isn't going to be able to support you and your younger staff safely into retirement, would you still try to inspire your people to dig deep?

All these questions are critical, and if we answer them correctly, it will naturally force us to an exponentially more faithful posture and presence in our communities. Your church may not live long, but I can guarantee that it will live better; and as God closes the doors on each ecclesial expression that comes and goes, people will thank you for the sacrifice you made.

Although many Christian leaders may choose to go the way of dementia and life in an assisted-living environment, we recommend that you stay lucid. You have some options. A well-planned life leads to an even more influential death, but you have to start that planning now.

DYING WELL

The issue of dying well has several critical factors.

1. Legacy must be motivated by real people. As inspiring as it may be to hand off the baton to the next generation of leaders, unless you have actual people whom you've come to love, pour time into, and be concerned about, you probably won't do what's necessary. As we write this, Matt is thirty-six and I am forty-two. This would normally be the time that we should be building a ministry that will carry us into our mid-fifties and beyond. Adullam is growing, and for the first time in five years, we could take close to full salaries, consolidate our trivocational life into one job, and take a bit of a breather. The problem is that we have seen God put before us Lou, Ryan, Dave, Laura, Mark, Jason, Julie, Julia, and Cory, and there are more behind them. These are young leaders whom we have come to not only love but feel responsible for. We see their gifting, their humility, their willingness to serve, and their hopes for a life of ministry and influence, but they can't get there on their own.

One of the aforementioned leaders shared with me a painful time when he asked his senior leadership to fund a two-day trip for him to get some leadership training. He was denied the opportunity because they said they couldn't afford it. A few days later, as he looked out his window, he saw that a dead thirty-foot palm tree was being replaced with a brand new thirty-foot tree. Out of curiosity, he walked over to the financial administrator's desk and inquired about the cost of the beautiful tree. He was told it was $10,000 dollars. We laughed about how that story stuck with him, but you could tell that it still hurt — that replacing a tree was a higher priority for the church leadership than contributing to his personal growth.

This generation is more than willing to be bivocational, but they still need a little help to even make that work. Seeing them struggle is what motivates Matt and me to enter their struggle with them. Do we lay up foundations and security for ourselves, or lay up treasures in heaven now? In John 4:34–38, Jesus is teaching his disciples about the hard work in the harvest field:

> "My food," said Jesus, "is to do the will of him who sent me and to finish his work. Do you not say, 'Four months more and then the harvest'? I tell you, open your eyes and look at the fields! They are ripe for harvest. Even now the reaper draws his wages, even now he harvests the crop for eternal life, so that the

sower and the reaper may be glad together. Thus the saying 'One sows and another reaps' is true. I sent you to reap what you have not worked for. Others have done the hard work, and you have reaped the benefits of their labor."

Here Jesus confirms two important facts. The first is, *it's time now!* No more waiting for the harvest. Stop saying, "after we get the building finished," or "once we reach 500 people," or "once we get out of the debt we're in," then we'll start preparing leadership for a church plant. The work of leadership development should not be an afterthought once we get our in-house stuff in order. It must be our priority at all times.

The second thing Jesus brings up is a reminder that the only reason any of us have had some sense of stability in ministry is because of someone else's labor. He's showing us the dependency we have on one another for the future of the church.

The plot thickens in Matthew 9:35–38:

Jesus went through all the towns and villages, teaching in their synagogues, proclaiming the good news of the kingdom and healing every disease and sickness. When he saw the crowds, he had compassion on them, because they were harassed and helpless, like sheep without a shepherd. Then he said to his disciples, "The harvest is plentiful but the workers are few. Ask the Lord of the harvest, therefore, to send out workers into his harvest field."

As I reflect on how I've responded to this Scripture, I realize that I've often missed the point. In times of fatigue or pressure to grow a church, I have often dropped to my knees and begged God to send me "helpers." I wanted God to give me people who would strengthen my ministry or lighten my load. My compassion was for myself. But this misses Jesus' point completely. It always seemed strange to me that Jesus was asking us to pray about something that he was already concerned about. Why didn't he just send leaders if he is really that uptight about the field? Why doesn't he generously fill our churches with hundreds of hard workers, gifted servants, and faithful leaders? The answer is that he has, but we're not as concerned about the bigger harvest as we need to be. They're there; we just won't release them, empower them, or serve their development at the level we need to. He includes us in his prayer because he is trying to tap us into the real issue of our hearts, our security, and our faith. That's what genuine prayer does. It gets us past strategy and into the substantive, sacred role of being a true kingdom leader.

So the first question you must ask yourself before you plan your legacy is, "*For whom* am I preparing it?" If we've only been preaching to a sea of nameless faces, it's easy to forget the power of what we do. Stop for a moment and think about actual individuals you hope would stand up at your funeral and say, "This person taught me how to live for Christ and to die with dignity." Hopefully this includes your children, maybe young men and women you've recruited into ministry, and maybe some whom you've spent years with mentoring, training, and coaching into who they are right now. Maybe it's even grandchildren or young kids who can't wait to see you. All these images should make this concept an emotionally charged quest.

2. Leave them something useful. Two weeks before my grandfather Leo died from heart issues, he invited me over. He didn't know it would be our last time together, but he must have sensed that he was getting close. He filled my truck full of tools, toolboxes, hardware, old baseball mitts, and yard tools. I was thrilled with all of these gifts, but then he took me upstairs to his gun closet and quietly handed me his 1956 Winchester lever-action .308 rifle. At the time, I was taken aback by his generosity.

A year later, I met Cheryl and began hunting with her family and was able to use the rifle. But over the years since my grandfather's passing, while I have used many of the things he gave me, many of the items were actually quite useless. The 400-pound 36-inch-blade chainsaw still runs, but the darn thing would take an NFL linebacker just to pull the cord, let alone pick up; the thirty chainsaw files don't serve my purposes since my new chainsaw comes with cheap replacement blades. Although they look cool hanging on a nail in my garage or sitting on a shelf, I have never needed the bark skinner, the grain sifter, or the meat grinder. And although I value all the items I was given, some are nostalgic — while others are used every week! So it is with the things we pass on.

Let me give you a few hints as to things that the next generation church leaders probably don't want or need from you: your building (if it carries a big mortgage), your debt, the unchurched culture's present level of disrespect and disdain for the church, and your parishioners' apathic consumer tendencies. Younger leaders won't want our iron-clad denominational loyalties, outdated ministerial codes of ethics, insensitive and unrealistic success measurements, or lengthy academic requirements that make them put real life and ministry on hold for a paper degree. They won't have much use for our massive wood pulpits, our pews, our individualistic communion trays, or our choir robes.

But here's what they do want from us: they will want your Bible commentaries and some use of your buildings, as long as it doesn't carry a lot of cost or control over their lives. Other than that, and a little cash, what they want most is your expertise, your mentoring, your encouragement, and a chance to hear the stories that will inform and inspire their leadership roles. They want tangible memories of how you modeled sacrifice, humility, teachability, risk, and courage in the face of ecclesial political pressure. They want to be inspired by how you gave away ministry, prestige, and power. They want to be entrusted with levels of responsibility that make them desperate for God's help. They want freedom to invent new ways of cultural engagement, discipleship, and teaching without being belittled if they fail. They want you to trust them to know how to reach their own generation. In short, they want a concerned but nurturing coach and someone after whom they can pattern their faith and leadership.

3. The biggest gift you can hand down is faith. During the week I was writing this chapter, I called a buddy, Phil Graf, who presently serves the cause of leadership development in Europe through Christian Associates. Phil has not only given huge lip service to the desperate need for leaders into Europe, but he has done so at huge risk and cost to his family. He moved from Oxnard to Amsterdam, and he is now moving his family to Portugal, all to create a leadership development center with the express goal of releasing 1001 new church leaders into the European context. I told him that Matt and I were at a crossroads between our own stability and the empowerment of our emerging leaders.

As we talked about the requirement of faith for our mutual commitments to create the baton and pass it down, as well as the personal cost associated with this, he shared these words: "Hugh, Adullam was started because you made a point to 'get in the way' of the lives of many people who did not know Christ. You intentionally blocked their paths of normal life and intentionally stayed in their way until they found God. Now, you must 'get out of the way' so that many more leaders will get in the way of the next wave."

We then talked about how this constant volley between being a leader and making leaders keeps us in a crucible of authentic faith. To that end, he added these thoughts. "Faith is easy when you can see around the bend in the road, when you know what's coming, where you're going, and what to do next. Faith is easy when you don't need it. And when you don't need it, it's not faith at all! Did Abraham know there was a ram caught in the thicket when he raised his knife in his outstretched arms high above the chest of his one and only son whom he loved so much? Did the boys in Daniel say, 'I'll get in the furnace if you, Lord, will turn down the heat!' Did Daniel ask the lion keeper, 'How hungry is this lion?' before he went into the cage? Did Moses know that he, and those families trusting his leadership, were going to escape the wrath of the furious Egyptian army as they walked across the dry bottom of the Red Sea?"

As we think about the rechurching of the West, we know that resources will be needed as never before—buildings will be appreciated for people to meet in; city-wide partnerships, network relationships, and training will be in high demand. They will need our best people resources, our best financial resources, and our best prayer resources. But one thing will be treasured above all of these things that we can pass down to our children's leaders and our grandchildren's leaders. It will be the most important thing we need to model and display for them: FAITH! Just as we are inspired by the writer of Hebrews to remember that cloud of witnesses, we, too, must become a cloud of witnesses who model faithful, sacrificial, faith-exploding leadership.

As ancient and modern Hebrews passed down the stories and sagas of their people's sacrifices and faith-filled exploits, the emerging leadership needs our stories. Stories of hospital visits, funerals, and tips for sermon prep? Not so much. They need stories of men and women who outgave, outfaithed, outrisked, outloved, and who got *out* of the way so they could get in the way. If we don't model it, they won't get it, and the ship will continue to take on water.

4. Peer pressure toward the right things. As we consider this new level of faith that leadership development will require, we'd like to suggest that we all may really need each other to stay true. In a short twenty years of church ministry, I can remember a lot of pastoral environments that actually created a peer pressure that went against this legacy mind-set. Conference after church planter conference, I felt more and more angst to grow my church, start my church, keep my leaders, and compete with the next guy. It's just built in. What we need is the new environment that we've been talking about. We need a new peer pressure that pushes us to think about our legacy more than impressing others in the present. Sometimes all you need to get over a faith barrier is to know that some other kingdom-minded knucklehead took the plunge of faith and sacrifice before you.

For instance, listen to Stephen Gray, who serves as a consultant to churches who wish to die well and sent this story:

Moon Lake General Baptist Church was started in 1990 by a group of Midwestern transfers. Their dream was to start a church that would provide stability and hope to a very dark area in New Port Richey. However, the majority of the congregation was past retirement and within ten years, the church found it impossible to continue supporting ministries essential for survival. It became evident to the congregation that closure was the only choice they had. So the leadership met and decided that in order to ensure the spread of the Gospel, they would give the property and assets to the Florida church planting board. Their one request that was that 100 percent of the money go to start a new congregation. While the amount given to the board was not great, it became foundational for New Walk Church in Zephyrhills, Florida.

On October 1, 2006, New Walk held its first service and welcomed over 350 people. Three years later, New Walk experienced over 1,100 in attendance, 350 first-time conversions to Christ, and 250 baptisms. The church has been recognized as one of the fast-growing new churches in the region. None of this would have been possible without the sacrifice and vision of the people from Moon Lake General Baptist Church. They decided to leave a legacy and hundreds now have a fresh start with God.

He also sent this story:

Charity Church, in the Little Rock metro area, had been around for over three decades. Once a growing congregation on the outer edges of the city, Charity Church soon found themselves overwhelmed by the onslaught of progressive suburban development. However, the congregants couldn't change quick enough to minister to the changing demographic, and they functioned much like they did thirty years earlier before they finally grew to understand that they had disconnected from their community. As the leadership of the church began to search for answers, more and more families left. It became painfully evident to those remaining that Charity Church would not last much longer. So, in the fall of 2006 they voted to close and pass on all assets and property to a new plant, Crossbridge Church in Bryant, Arkansas, set to launch in Sept 2007. The congregation had served four decades of believers during its life.

Here's an inspiring list of stories we've seen over the last few years:

⇨ Alex Early: Four Corners Church, Georgia, graduate of Oxford, 28, a mega-church, everything man for three years; realized that he and Jesus had nothing in common, religious people loved him and pagans hated him, so he quit, got a job at a bar as a stock boy, ended up planting a church two years later based around the "Alamo Bar." Now running two services from the Alamo.

⇨ Portland church of 500 people with 12 staff all committed to give up their expense accounts, pool the savings, and support 3 intern level positions each year.

⇨ Mega-church pastor Tom in Phoenix, who has been leading the congregation he started twenty years ago while not taking a salary, so that other young leaders could be on staff.

⇨ Harold in Edmonton, who left a mega-church role to start a network of neighborhood-based communities. His motto is work 9 to 5, plant a church 5 to 9. He sells cars to make ends meet.

⇨ Gary, Seth, Gerry, Mike, Jim, Don, and Nick — a small number of men we've met who had faithfully pastored local churches for many years, but who (like Lance Armstrong and the Tour de France) decided to come out of retirement and reenter the world of church planting, giving up a sure salary and a safe reputation. All of these men are over forty-five.

⇨ Kevin, who has been a denominational church plant director, and who felt he could lead best by modeling. He realized that his denominational-based salary could support two church planters a year and so he continued to serve as a catalyst, encourager, and trainer on his spare time while he reentered the harvest to plant another church.

⇨ Free-Methodist River Conference, committing $100,000 to a local church plant ministry that was completely unaffiliated with them, just because they wanted to see something happen.

⇨ A Denver church deciding to sell their building, build a smaller one with cash, and then commit the profit to new church works.

Can you feel yourself thinking outside the box? Can you sense the beauty of God's *sent* church filling your lungs with kingdom air again? God's heroes are everywhere, and we need to find them and rub up against them so we can learn to be like them. The resources for the emerging church is in the hands of the existing church. We have everything they will need. Will we release it? Will we release them?

FINAL THOUGHTS FROM HUGH

Here's a final thought that I live with daily. The very moment I stop breathing, I will see the face of Jesus. It could be forty years from now, or it could be today at 7:42 p.m. At that moment, all impure motives, self-oriented exploits, and fleshly ventures will be burned away like chaff. I'm not sure if he will show a movie reel or just let me see my life as a reflection in his eyes, but what I hope to see are the things I did that represented him well, made him proud, and legitimately served his kingdom cause. I've settled the issue that success is not what I'll be worried about in that moment. The real question will be my faithfulness to do what he has called me to do and how closely I followed his lead.

The essence of the Christian faith is that our God intentionally came to lay down his life as a ransom for all. It was a necessary tragedy that brought life. And his kamikaze mission had a clear target: you and me. His teaching and way of life and his call to the church speaks as a clarion call to each of us to give our lives away. Hear again his words to his would-be leaders.

⇨ "If anyone wants to be first, he must be the very last, and the servant of all" (Mark 9:35).

⇨ "Whoever wants to save his life will lose it, but whoever loses his life for me and for the gospel will save it" (Mark 8:35).

⇨ "I tell you the truth, unless a kernel of wheat falls to the ground and dies, it remains only a single seed. But if it dies, it produces many seeds" (John 12:24).

Later, other followers and leaders like Paul used phrases like these:

⇨ "Even if I am to be poured out as a drink offering on the sacrifice and service coming from your faith, I am glad and rejoice" (Phil. 2:17).

If spiritual leadership is anything, it is a journey *of* death and a journey *to* death. One journey is an inward dying to ourselves, our concerns, our ambitions, and our pride, and the other is a preparation for our actual, physical death, where the only thing that matters is what we've left to those who will follow us.

We hope that in this simple story of the AND, you have found some renewed hope in God's plan for the church. Although we don't feel as if we've given you any wildly new thoughts, we trust that what we've been seeing and hearing out in the field will encourage you in the unique calling you have to help lead, serve, and die in God's church worldwide. This beautifully sent and gathered church cost Jesus his very life, and it is certainly worth our very best efforts.

Peace Out

Hugh and Matt

Share Your Thoughts

With the Author: Your comments will be forwarded to the author when you send them to *zauthor@zondervan.com*.

With Zondervan: Submit your review of this book by writing to *zreview@zondervan.com*.

Free Online Resources at
www.zondervan.com

Zondervan AuthorTracker: Be notified whenever your favorite authors publish new books, go on tour, or post an update about what's happening in their lives at www.zondervan.com/authortracker.

Daily Bible Verses and Devotions: Enrich your life with daily Bible verses or devotions that help you start every morning focused on God. Visit www.zondervan.com/newsletters.

Free Email Publications: Sign up for newsletters on Christian living, academic resources, church ministry, fiction, children's resources, and more. Visit www.zondervan.com/newsletters.

Zondervan Bible Search: Find and compare Bible passages in a variety of translations at www.zondervanbiblesearch.com.

Other Benefits: Register yourself to receive online benefits like coupons and special offers, or to participate in research.